MAKING
FELT BAGS

as if you need
another book
on feltmaking!

with best wishes

Mandy

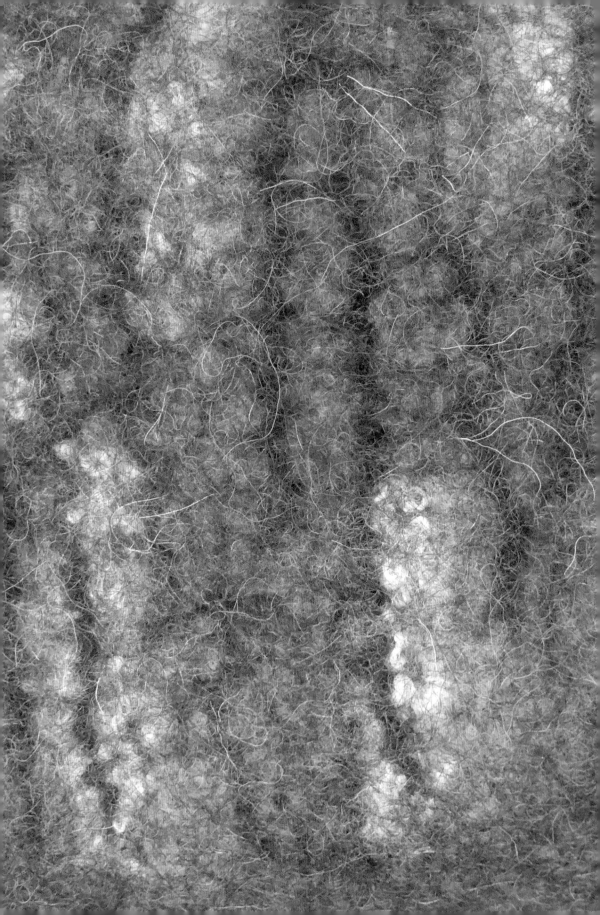

MAKING
FELT BAGS

Mandy Nash

CROWOOD

First published in 2021 by
The Crowood Press Ltd
Ramsbury, Marlborough
Wiltshire SN8 2HR

enquiries@crowood.com
www.crowood.com

British Library Cataloguing-in-Publication Data
A catalogue record for this book is available from the British Library.

ISBN 978 1 78500 862 7

Acknowledgements
I have my grandmothers, Alice and Muriel, to thank for starting me off on my creative journey, passing on their traditional textile skills with boundless patience. My parents have to take some credit too, with their non-judgmental attitude towards my career choice and constant support and encouragement.

A special thank you must go to Heather Potten. An exceptional proof reader, she ensured that the content was understandable. Thanks too, to Eva Leslie, Jenny Rolfe and Jackie Stringer for double checking the text.

I must credit Heidi McEvoy-Swift for inventing the shrinkage test sample in Chapter 3, which is such an invaluable teaching aid. Thank you to all the feltmakers, whose workshops I have attended over the years, who have been generous in passing on their knowledge; to my students too, who have encouraged me to develop my skills. A special mention must go to Jenny Pepper for helping me to understand how to use a resist and Heidi Greb for introducing me to using raw fleece.

The lovely photographs of the finished bags were taken by Kate Stuart
www.katestuartphotography.com

Typeset by Sharon Dainton Design
Printed and bound in India by Replika Press Pvt. Ltd.

CONTENTS

INTRODUCTION

I first encountered felt in the 1980s when I saw the work of Annie Sherburne. I bought one of her kits and made some 'interesting' samples with an unknown variety of wool that was tricky to felt. I only slightly fell in love with the technique then, rolling with my feet in my mother's kitchen and not fully understanding the process but loving the result. Roll on almost twenty years. Kate Bosset, a friend who had recently discovered feltmaking at a convergence in New Zealand (and had sought tuition from Anne Belgrave on her return to the UK), reacquainted me with the craft, as 'I would love feltmaking.' She was right. I bought some merino roving which sat in my studio for three months until I eventually struggled to interpret my scant notes, remember what she had taught me, and make some rather strange felt samples. I was hooked.

I trained as a jeweller and continue to make my living from making and selling jewellery. My work has been heavily influenced by both traditional and contemporary textiles. My three passions are colour, pattern and technique. I love making things and exploring the possibilities of different materials. I use non-traditional materials to make my jewellery, which is highly colourful and often incorporates either textiles or textile techniques. Feltmaking contrasts with and complements jewellery making so it is the perfect marriage – I enjoy working in both crafts. My feltmaking journey has had to fit in with making a living from selling my jewellery, attending the occasional workshop to extend my meagre knowledge alongside endless sessions making samples, often unsuccessfully as my ambitions exceeded my skills. The act of feltmaking is slow but meditative and cannot be rushed. In contrast with the insular nature of making jewellery, it is a sociable activity; you can make felt with people. My journey continues, as there is so much to learn about felt and its unique properties.

I have often been asked for recommendations for a good book for a feltmaking beginner to buy. It is a difficult question to answer – the longer I make felt, the more I realize what a diverse medium it is and there are constantly new developments. As finding one book to cover all of this is impossible, I refer to several books for technical reference and many more in a much broader area for inspiration. Each feltmaker works in a different way, and the way one works is also dependent on what one is making. There is never only one solution.

My aim for this book is to provide an all-round guide and instruction manual to making functional felt bags for all levels of experience. It covers the principles of using a resist to create three-dimensional forms, looks at the shapes and styles of bags to suit all occasions and works with a variety of wool breeds. Each step-by-step project expands on the earlier chapters to explain and explore the processes of design and making to produce bags fit for purpose. To fully understand these processes, read the whole book before you start. There is never an end as there is always something new to discover.

MATERIALS AND EQUIPMENT

Read this chapter before rushing to buy any wool or equipment. There is an immense amount of information to absorb initially, which will gradually become relevant once you start to make felt. If you understand the materials you are working with, your feltmaking journey will be speedier and your finished products more professional.

WOOL: YOUR CHOSEN MATERIAL

Wool is a natural, sustainable resource with excellent thermal qualities and many uses. Felt is one of the earliest known textiles and is not necessarily made from wool – it can be made from various animal hair fibres such as alpaca, mohair, cashmere, camel, rabbit and beaver. However, wool felts best without the aid of any harmful chemicals.

Animal fibres felt together as their surface is covered in scales, smooth one way and rough the other. When moisture, heat and friction are applied, the scales soften, open up and link together to form a strong and versatile fabric. There are many varieties of sheep and their wool quality varies from thick and coarse for hardy sheep living in harsh climates to fine and soft such as merino that can survive in hotter weather. The length of the fibres (staple), the hardness of the scales on the fibres plus the crimp (curl) affect the ability of the wool to felt. Usually, wools with a long staple and good crimp felt well.

When I first discovered feltmaking, I had not realized that there were so many varieties of sheep, each with a delightful, fluffy wrapper. The wool of each breed of sheep has its own distinct properties. Some breeds felt well and quickly; some more slowly and with more effort; and some not at all. The quality and feel of the felt produced also varies tremendously. Some sheep are bred for meat only and their fleece does not usually make good felt. However, in the interests of limiting waste, other uses are being sought, such as insulation and slug repellent.

Like most beginners, I originally started making felt with merino wool, as it felts easily and is universally available in a good range of colours. As my fascination with making felt developed, so did my interest in the different varieties of wool. Opting to use just merino seriously limits the range of work you can produce. It is worthwhile experimenting and making samples with different breeds of wool to understand their characteristics, helping you to choose the correct breed to suit the purpose of your project. Merino might not necessarily be your first choice for making a bag. As a general rule, use a finer wool for making garments or items that are worn next to the skin that need to drape, and a coarser wool for items that need to be strong and hard-wearing,

Left: An assortment of wools.

such as a bag.

There are too many sheep breeds to mention in this book, and each country has regional varieties. The effort involved in sampling different breeds will expand your felt-making skills, save you time in the long run and help you decide which wool to use for your felt projects. Understanding the characteristics of different sheep breeds will make you a better feltmaker. If you are interested in the history of feltmaking, you will find further reading in the reference section at the end of this book.

The characteristics of wool are described as a) thickness and length of fibre, b) lustre and c) crimp (waviness). The measurement in microns refers to the thickness of the fibre (the lower the number, the finer the wool) and the staple is the length of the fibre. Generally, the thicker wool with a longer staple produces a coarser and more hard-wearing felt. However, each wool has its individual characteristics (even within the same breed, depending on age, diet and climate). Some may contain thicker kemp fibres, produce a hairy finish, feel springy or lofty or have some elasticity. Others may felt really firmly, or be compact or loose. Wool with a good lustre and crimp usually felts well. If it is smooth, lacking lustre and crimp and has an even staple, it does not.

Natural wool (undyed) has a different feel, as it has not been through the harsh, chemical dyeing process and the subtle colour variations are not to be ignored in preference to the instant appeal of the multitude of colours available in dyed wool.

The more you felt, the more you will discover about this fascinating medium.

Unwashed fleece

Wool directly shorn from the sheep is dirty and will need to be cleaned to remove the dirt,

dust and grease and then combed and carded so all the fibres lie in the same direction. Washing and carding fleece is a labour-intensive and physical activity and not an essential task for a feltmaker. I recommend starting with off-the-shelf, cleaned, combed and carded, pre-dyed or natural fleece.

If you are offered a whole dirty fleece fresh from the sheep, think twice before accepting it especially if you are unsure of the breed (it may not even be a good felter) or are not going to clean and card it straightaway. Dirty fleece deteriorates and attracts moths more than clean fleece.

Wool can be purchased in the form of roving (tops) and batts. A batt is lifted directly from the carding machine as loose fibres. If the batt is then combed so that the fibres are all in the same direction, it becomes a roving – a continuous rope of wool. Most wool comes in the form of roving. I will explain how to use both batts and roving in the next chapter.

Some colourful, merino wool. I try to keep similar kinds of fleece together so I can identify them easily. I store my most frequently used wool in underbed boxes so I can see the range of colours at a glance.

WOOL BREEDS FOR FELTING

WOOL BREED/TYPE	ORIGIN	THICKNESS (MICRONS)	STAPLE (MM)	COMMENTS
Bergschaf	Austria	35–45	100–200	This is one of my favourite wools as it felts like a dream and produces a strong-wearing felt that does not pill. Some find it a little hairy. The German Bergschaf translates as 'mountain sheep', a generic term. The best wool comes from the Tyrolean region.
Black Welsh	UK	31–35	80–100	The only black fleece in the UK, it felts well, producing a strong spongy felt which is good for making bags.
Blue-faced Leicester	UK	26	85–90	This is a lovely wool with a good crimp and lustre. It is very soft so perfect for garments but suitable for making bags too, as it is slightly stronger than merino.
Corriedale	Australia, New Zealand, South Africa and North and South America	25–30	75–120	This wool is slightly coarser than merino and also available in a range of colours. It has a good crimp and felts well so is suitable for larger bags.
Finn wool	Finland	28–30	80	This makes a strong felt ideal for making bags and comes in a range of natural colours. There are various sources of this wool (it is a generic term) and the quality varies too.
Gotland	Scandinavia	30–34	80–150	A lovely soft and lustrous wool which felts very well.
Icelandic wool	Iceland	34–36	90–100	This felts in a similar way to Finn wool but is a little hairy. Again, it is a generic description so the quality varies.
Manx Loaghtan	UK	29–31	75–80	A very rare, old breed found in the Isle of Man. It is a gorgeous, chocolate-brown colour and is similar to Black Welsh. It is suitable for smaller bags and can be rather spongy.
Masham	UK	38–44	150–380	This produces a strong felt which is a little hairy.
Merino	Australia, New Zealand, South Africa and South America	14.5–25.5	75–80	Available in a wide range of colours and qualities – use the finer for garments, the thicker for bags. It felts well but needs to be fulled sufficiently to produce a hard-wearing surface, otherwise it is liable to pill. Suitable for smaller bags that will not attract too much hard wear.
New Zealand	New Zealand	30–32	90–110	This wool is very similar to Corriedale. It has a good crimp and felts well but is rather soft so is suitable for smaller bags.
Norwegian	Norway	33–36	80–120	One of the older sheep breeds that felts well for a strong finish. It can feel a bit spongy.
Shetland	UK	29–31	90	This wool comes in a lovely selection of natural colours. It felts well and produces a strong finish whilst remaining soft.
Swaledale	UK	35–45	100–200	The fleece used to produce carpet yarn, varying in colour from white to grey. It felts surprisingly well, producing a hard-wearing felt suitable for larger bags.
Wensleydale	UK	40–50	200–300	This wool has a very long staple and has a wonderful lustre. It makes a lovely filigree felt which is suitable for garments but can be used with other wools to create great texture. A fine layer works well over yarn patterns to hold them in place.
Zwartbles	Netherlands	30–32	100–120	This has an excellent crimp and produces a good strong felt.

Storing wool

It is tempting to overbuy when you start felt-making and you will soon end up with a large stash. Try to avoid this, if possible. Storing wool takes up space while repeated handling of wool will matt or felt it, making it harder to use and providing a home for moths. Keeping your wool in cloth bags is best as it allows it to breathe and prevents condensation. Try to adopt a methodical method of storing your wool; keep the same varieties together and label them clearly. Although some wools are easy to identify, many are very similar. Being organized will save time in the long run and make it easy to select the correct materials for a project.

On the previous page are suggestions of suitable wool breeds readily available in the UK. Do compare and try out your regional wools as well. Later in the book, I will explain the wool choices for each project.

Moths

It is best to buy your wool from a reputable supplier. If you have been given wool or fibre second-hand, keep it in your freezer for three to four weeks to kill any eggs. If you have freezer space, it is worth rotating and storing your wool in this way to break the breeding cycle. A chest freezer in your garage or shed is the perfect solution if you have the space. There are various products available to either deter or kill moths. Take care to follow instructions if you use any that contain harmful chemicals. For a safer approach, you may choose to use sandalwood, lavender or bay leaves, which can deter moths but not kill them. Regular checking and rotating your stash of wool is recommended to keep the creatures in check.

EQUIPMENT

A major attraction of feltmaking is that it does not require expensive equipment. Although specialist equipment is available, you might not necessarily need it, as it is easy to adapt tools you already own. Charity shops are a rich source of handy implements, such as wooden and plastic massagers. I will explain my own feltmaking techniques and why I choose to work the way I do. However, each feltmaker develops their own working methods; once you understand each stage of the feltmaking process, you can select the appropriate tools to help you achieve the desired result.

The following describes the equipment I use. You will not need all these items when you start out; I have accumulated them over time.

Ribbed rubber mat

I work on a ribbed rubber mat as a working surface for several reasons: it protects the table I am working on; it provides a non-slip surface for rolling; and you can work directly on it once you move onto the final, fulling phase of feltmaking. It is also great for making cords as, again, you can work directly on the mat. You can find suitable materials at DIY centres sold as non-slip matting. Some drawer liners have a ribbed texture which also works well. It also obviates the need to work on a towel, which can become wet very quickly and drip water on the floor.

Plastic bowls

A selection of plastic bowls in different sizes will be useful for your spray and soap, for warming felt, for catching drips, and for transporting wet felt. (Breakable ones are not suitable, as they are easily dropped, especially when handling with soapy hands.)

My table ready to start work. I am an untidy person, so I try to select only the tools I need for the project in hand in order to have adequate space to work.

Sponges, cloths and towels

Sponges are essential for mopping up any excess water, and you will find having one or two super-absorbent cloths to hand will be very useful too, especially for removing excess water from your work. Three or four old towels are all one requires when working directly on a rubber mat. A small one is handy too for drying hands between laying and wetting down the wool.

Rolling mats

Over the years, I have experimented with different ways of working. I now lay out the wool directly onto a non-slip mat such as the ones that are used under rugs. These are light, washable, reusable and dry quickly. I occasionally use a bamboo mat when fulling or making cords. These attract mould if not fully dried before storing and they can be tough on your hands too. You can also use bubble wrap, cotton sheeting, thin plastic dust sheet or a towel to roll your work. I use all of these from time to time depending on what I am making – this will be explained in later chapters.

Ties

You may wish to tie your work up when rolling so a set of ties are required. These can be anything from elastic bands, cut-up tights, T-shirts or plastic bags to ribbon, string, hair scrunchies or elastic.

Pipe cladding and dowelling

You will need something to roll your work around – I use foam pipe cladding but swimming pool noodles or a rolled-up towel or bubble wrap will also suffice. For the final fulling, wooden dowelling is useful too. I have pipe cladding and dowelling in a range of sizes to fit the size of work I am making.

Soap

There is much debate about what soap is suitable for making felt – each feltmaker will defend their choice. Some make their own soap solutions; however, I go for the simplest option. I use a teaspoon of liquid soap flakes (available from most supermarkets) in a bowl of hand-hot water for wetting down. When extra soap is required when working with my hands or tools, I use an olive oil soap. I find this soap leaves my hands soft and supple. I suffer with allergies from other soap products but have no problem with a good brand of olive oil soap.

Sprinkler ball

To wet down the wool after laying down, I use a sprinkler ball, which can also be known as a ball brause sprinkler or felting bulb spray. This is the one felting item that I would recommend buying – I would be lost without mine! A plastic bottle with holes drilled in the top will serve the same purpose. Some felters use spray bottles too, but if these are too fierce, they can move your carefully laid down fibres.

A selection of tools that every feltmaker should possess. Good sharp scissors are essential plus a pair for cutting paper and plastic.

Felting tools

There are many specially designed felting tools on the market now. When I first started making felt, there were none, so I have collected and made a range of items that work for me. Wooden tools can be extremely useful for shaping. These include darning mushrooms, garden dibbers, rolling pins, spoons and odd pieces of dowelling. Many of these can be found in charity shops alongside various devices for massaging the body which some felters find really handy. One extremely useful home-made tool that I use frequently is a small block of wood with a drawer handle attached on the top covered with ribbed floor protector plastic on the bottom, held in place by staples around the edges.

In an effort to keep everything tidy, I store all my small feltmaking kit in this portable set of drawers. Note the bed risers which lift my table to the correct height for working.

My collection of devices that I use for rubbing and forming. Some are purpose-made for feltmaking but many have been adapted, such as the dibber and wooden fork. Charity shops can be a source for odd bits of equipment such as small back massagers.

Bed risers

These are useful to ensure that your table is the right height for you to work comfortably. They are normally used for raising chairs and beds for the elderly and disabled and are economical, easily transportable and available in a range of heights.

Resist material

I use thin PVC table covering sold by the metre, which is just the right thickness; thick enough for feeling the edge when wrapping the wool and thin enough to shrink with the

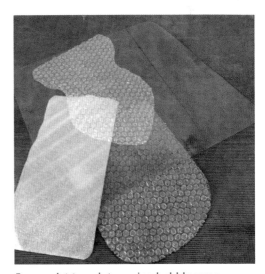

Four resist templates using bubble wrap, laminate floor underlay and plastic table covering.

wool without stretching the fibres. I sometimes use bubble wrap (I would not recommend this for beginners as it is harder to feel
the edges) and laminate floor underlay (which
can tear).

Spin dryer

A small free-standing one is very handy to
speed up the drying process, especially as
many modern washing machines do not have
a controllable spin cycle. You can usually find
second-hand ones to buy. Some feltmakers use
washing machines to felt their work but I prefer to be in total control of the process, which
can only be truly assessed by touch.

Surface decoration

Materials that can be incorporated with wool
will be fully explained in the chapter on decoration. As with your wool, store all extra 'bits
and bobs' in a logical manner. I use clear plastic boxes so I can easily identify the contents. I
waste nothing and have boxes of yarn, fabric
scraps and pre-felts.

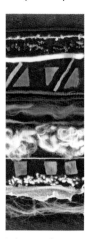

**It is worth experimenting with decorative
elements as they are dramatically transformed
once felted.**

Other useful items

Bubble wrap: to wet down the wool. I keep a
range of sizes for different uses.
Netting: useful for wetting down.
Plastic bags: also useful for wetting down and
for polishing your finished items.
Disposable plastic gloves: very handy for rubbing your work, especially if you have sensitive
skin or do not like the feel of soap on your
hands. Also good for polishing your finished
items.
Scissors: you will need a minimum of three
pairs – embroidery (sharp with pointed ends –
absolutely essential), a larger pair (ideally
dressmaking scissors) and an ordinary pair for
cutting paper.
Needles and thread: the thread should be
colourfast, and strong enough not to snap
when put under pressure.
Plastic dust sheet: the thin kind has several
uses: as a protector to hold your surface decoration in place; to use as a resist material; and
to create neat edges.
Ruler: several lengths are useful for measuring
and designing resist templates, calculating
shrinkage and placing your decoration.
Permanent felt tip pens: to mark out your
resist templates.
Tape measure
Digital scales: invaluable for weighing your
wool to ensure you lay the wool evenly.
Newspaper/scrap paper: for sketching out
templates and padding out your finished
pieces to keep their shape.
Watercolour pencils and pencil sharpeners:
for marking out your work.
Forceps: very useful for retrieving resists from
small holes and straightening and pulling
edges into shape.
Felting needles and sponge: useful for quick
repairs.
Masking tape: in different widths, for holding
resists in place and to use as a resist.

HEALTH AND SAFETY

Making felt is good for your health and mental well-being – it is a good, physical activity. However, do consider the following:

• Ensure that the tables you use are the correct height using bed risers if necessary. I prefer to work standing as I can access the whole of the work easily (especially working on larger items) and I am not hunched over the work. You can also use the whole of your body when rolling.

• If you prefer to sit when working, stand up regularly and stretch.

• Try to alternate your actions so as not to use repetitive movements. Take regular breaks and stretch.

• You may find it easier to stand with your legs apart and bent when rolling, using the whole length of your arms and wrists and the weight of your body.

• If you have sensitive skin, wearing gloves (the thinner plastic variety rather than the latex ones) can be very useful, and they can be reused. Regular use of hand cream helps keep your hands smooth when handling the wool, to prevent catching.

• Be careful and take necessary precautions when using hot water. I use a microwave to heat my work rather than boiling water as it heats the whole item and there is less danger of scalding. Do use protective gloves when required.

• Carry wet work around in a bowl so you are not leaving a trail of water on the floor where you could slip – mop up any spills straight away.

• Ensure that you wash your hands thoroughly after using unwashed fleece.

THE BASICS OF FELTMAKING

If you have not made any felt before, then it is important to learn the basics before embarking on a project. An understanding of the material that you are working with will pay dividends later and enable you to take on the challenge of working with a resist and designing your bags with ease. Feltmaking is a labour-intensive activity, so it is essential not to waste time by trying to run before you can walk; this will result in frustration when your project does not meet your expectations. Patience pays off. I wholeheartedly recommend you make a series of samples in different wools, varying the number of layers, to observe the differences in texture, feel and shrinkage. Do not assume that all wools work in the same way – you will be surprised at the differences. As with all crafts, your skills will improve the more you practise, so the process becomes instinctive.

Even if you have some feltmaking experience, please read this chapter. Make a few samples in the wools you like to use, as these will be necessary in calculating the correct shrinkage for your chosen designs. There is no one simple formula for making felt. It all depends on what you are making, taking into account the size and function of your design and what wool you are using. Each feltmaker works in a different way; these are the techniques that I use, which work for me. Once you understand the process, you can experiment and develop your own methods.

PREPARATION

When taking the first steps in feltmaking, keep everything to a small scale to speed up your learning. Start with a 20cm (8in) square; it is a manageable size to lay out and felt and it makes it easier to calculate the shrinkage. I use a 20cm (8in) square template; make this in plastic so you can reuse it – paper templates tend to get wet and tear.

To make your samples, you will need the following equipment as explained in Chapter 1:

• Mat or towel to work on
• Noodle
• Soap
• Bowl
• Spray or water bottle
• Sponge
• Small piece of bubble wrap
• Small non-slip mat or bubble wrap
• Wool
• Scales
• A spare towel to dry your hands

Left: By changing the size and shape of the resist template and varying the wool, a myriad of designs can be created.

Get everything you need ready before you start. You can then work without interruptions and concentrate fully on the task in hand. As you are only working on a small scale, you may wish to work sitting down. If not, make sure that your table is the correct height so as not to harm your back or shoulders.

MAKING SAMPLES

I recommend making the following samples (all starting with a 20cm (8in) square) so you can compare the quality and feel of the wool. These will also be invaluable when you move onto the design stage and need to calculate shrinkage for your project:

1. A four-layer sample using merino roving
2. A six-layer sample in merino roving
3. A four-layer sample in a coarser wool roving such as Corriedale, Shetland, Icelandic, Zwartbles, Masham
4. A six-layer sample in a coarser wool such as Corriedale, Shetland, Icelandic, Zwartbles, Masham

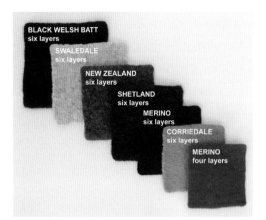

Laying your samples side by side illustrates the different shrinkage rates. Label your samples for future reference – do not rely on your memory!

5. A four-layer sample using wool in batt such as Bergschaf, Finn wool, Black Welsh
6. A six-layer sample using wool in batt such as Bergschaf, Finn wool, Black Welsh

Once you have mastered the technique of making samples, experiment with mixing different breeds of wool to observe how the texture and feel changes.

Beginners tend to lay out their wool quite thickly until they master the technique of

SOAP, WATER TEMPERATURE AND WETTING DOWN

I use approximately a teaspoon of liquid soap flakes in a bowl of hand-hot water. The warmth of the water and the soap will help open the scales on the wool so it will felt. Some coarser wools will take more wetting down to open the scales. If the wool has not soaked up any water and looks 'fluffy', it will not felt. I wet down every two layers for two reasons: you use less water as the water from the bottom layers permeates through the upper layers, and there is less movement in the wool. Some wools spread considerably after wetting; this varies from breed to breed.

Do not use very hot water with the initial wetting down or you will start the felting process too soon – at this stage you just want to open the scales on the wool fibres. Do not use too much soap, as the soap bubbles will prevent the wool fibres from felting. For this reason, I never use liquid detergent (it is also extremely harsh on your hands).

You might wish to make a soap solution by grating olive oil soap and adding hot water to make a syrup. You can then mix a spoonful of this in a bowl of hand-hot water. To avoid clogging up your spray bottle, ensure that the soap has dissolved fully.

holding the wool and pulling even tufts. Finer layers make a much better and stronger felt, so it is good practice to weigh the wool in order to control the thickness you are laying down. You will need approximately 2.5g per layer so you will require 10g for a four-layer sample and 15g for a six-layer sample. This will help you lay down the wool evenly. You might struggle at first but do persevere. Weigh your wool before you start; it is much easier to handle when your hands are dry before you start felting and they get wet. Weigh out the total amount, then divide the roving into two, which helps you to lay down the wool finely. If you are a total beginner, split the wool into the number of layers you wish to use so you have even layers. With practice, you will no longer need to do this as it will become instinctive.

Laying down roving

This takes practice, so do not panic if your first attempt is not perfect; you will improve. Wool is an incredibly strong medium – try holding the roving with a small gap between your hands and pulling – it will not break however hard you pull. As you move your hands further apart, you will be able to pull off a tuft or shingle. Depending on the length of the staple of the wool you are working with, the distance will vary. To make sure that your length of roving is even, you might need to tease it out before you start. You will find it easier to lay out your fibre if you split your roving equally into two along its length.

Hold the wool fibres at the very tip of the roving across its entire width with one hand. With your other hand hold the roving 10–20cm (4–8in) further down and pull off a shingle (tuft). Your shingle should be even – if you hold the wool too far down the roving or pick it off with your fingers, it will be too thick and uneven. The more you practise, the more even your shingles

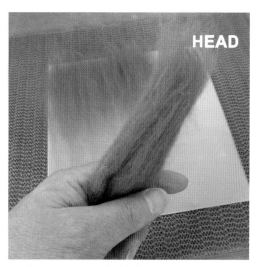

It takes practice to hold the roving correctly. Try to hold it evenly and not bunch it up in your hand.

will become. You will find some wools are easier to lay down than others; merino, especially, if it is not fresh from the supplier, can become stringy and harder to lay down evenly.

The top of the shingle I will call the 'head' and the bottom the 'tail'. The head has a straighter edge whereas the tail is wispier. This can be used advantageously – if you place the head on the edge of your work it will form a neater edge and

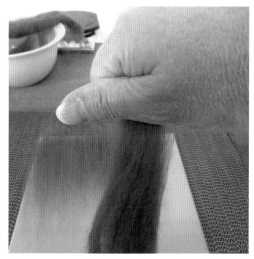

Grip the wool right at the top of the roving and hold firmly before pulling a shingle.

the tail is useful when using several colours to achieve a softer, blended join.

The wool shrinks in the direction of the staple, which is why an even number of layers is necessary and are placed at right angles to each other in order for your work to shrink proportionally. Directional shrinkage can be exploited to create form and shape, which is especially useful when making garments. However, when making bags, even shrinkage is necessary.

PROJECT ▶ MAKING A SQUARE SAMPLE USING ROVING

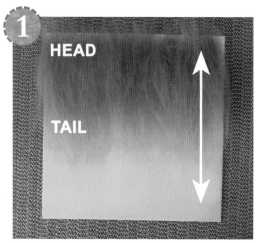

HEAD

TAIL

Place your plastic square on your non-slip mat or bubble wrap. Pull a shingle and place with the 'head' to the top of the square. Lay a row of shingles across the top, overlapping as if you are tiling a roof.

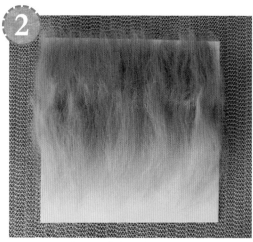

Lay a second row of shingles, placing the 'head' of the second row over the 'tail' of the first row.

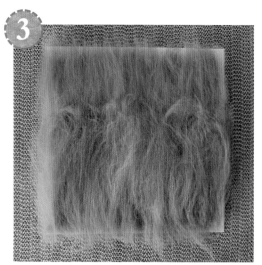

Lay the third row of shingles with the 'head' on the bottom edge and the 'tails' of the second and third rows overlapping.

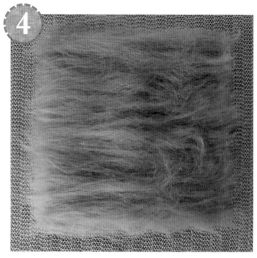

The second layer of shingles is placed at right angles to the first layer, as in steps 1 to 3. Pat the wool down and even out if necessary.

Wet the wool gently with warm, soapy water so as not to disturb the fibres. Use the water sparingly – it is best to add more if necessary, rather than flood your piece. If your fibres are 'floating', they will be too far apart to felt.

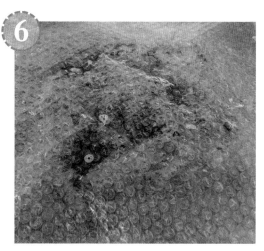

Cover the sample in bubble wrap with the bubble side down and sprinkle a little soapy water on top. This prevents the bubble wrap from slipping and moving your fibres. Gently press down to spread the water through the fibres, then rub gently – a similar action to rubbing a dog's tummy.

You need to ensure that all the fibres are wet. They will darken if wet through and should not appear fluffy. Add more water if necessary. Repeat steps 1 to 7 for layers 3 and 4. If you are laying down 6 layers, then repeat again.

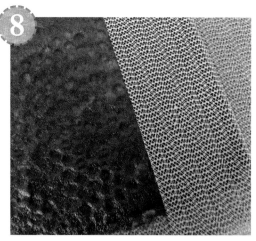

To neaten edges, fold over the stray fibres. Use your mat and the hard edge of the plastic square to do this.

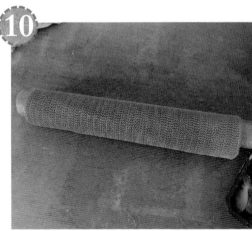

Repeat on all four sides; if you have excess fibre in the corners, form a mitre and cut off. Fold the mat over the sample and, holding your work firmly with the mat, turn it over. Remove your plastic square template, taking care not to lift the fibres.

With the mat or bubble wrap sandwiching your sample, roll around the noodle loosely. You can tie the roll with rubber bands, tape or hair scrunchies to prevent the roll from unwinding, although when working on a small scale, this might not be necessary. Rest your hands on top and gently roll fifty times. Unwind your roll and turn 90 degrees clockwise and roll another fifty times. Repeat twice more to complete a 360-degree rotation. As the wool shrinks in the direction you are rolling, it is important that you treat each side equally.

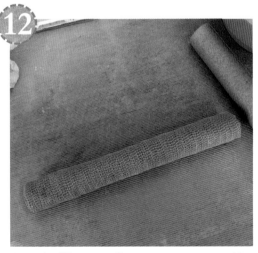

Making sure that you have gripped your work securely, flip over and repeat step 10. The wool fibres should now appear settled and look more like a fabric. If the fibres still look loose (if you pinch them and they lift easily), roll with the noodle for a little longer.

Once the fibres are all secure, repeat steps 10 and 11 without the noodle.

Your sample should now have shrunk considerably and the fibres should be well matted and should not move when you rub your fingers over the surface. If not, roll for a little longer.

It may look as though you have finished felting at this stage but your sample needs fulling and finishing so it will endure the wear and tear of a bag. If left at this point, the felt will become fluffy and pill very quickly. Rub some soap over both sides of the sample to prevent the fibres from lifting.

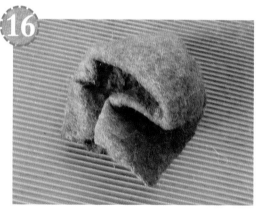

Roll directly on the rubber mat, a ribbed surface or in a bamboo mat, rotating the sample and turning over, treating each side equally so it shrinks uniformly.

Apply more soap (this prevents the fibres from lifting and making the piece hairy), then massage it in your hands. You can also throw it on your mat twenty to fifty times. Warm the sample either by heating it in a microwave or plunging in a bowl of hot water and repeat steps 15 and 16.

Continue to massage, throw and roll the sample (reheating it when it cools down) until it no longer shrinks. Roll it firmly around a wooden dowel or piece of hard plastic for a smooth finish.

You can further neaten the edges by rolling them. If a section needs more shrinking, such as a corner, just work on that area by rolling or rubbing. Rolling will give a smoother finish to the surface, whilst throwing forces the fibre to migrate adding to the texture.

Wool is incredibly strong and, when wet, can be pulled into shape. Stretch your piece to make it square and tug at the edges to make them straight. You can use a pair of forceps or pliers to do this. Rinse your piece thoroughly to remove all the soap. You can rub with a piece of thin plastic or a plastic bag to polish the surface to smooth the fibres. Pull into shape and leave to dry flat. This is important as felt has a memory and will retain its shape.

ROLLING

Everyone's rolling action varies so it is not easy to specify how long or how many rolls you need, and it depends on what you are making. By rolling, you are applying friction to the wool fibres to encourage the scales to open and the fibres to intertwine together. It is important to start gently (you are not rolling pastry or trying to squeeze out the water), applying very light pressure and moving your hands along the work using a rocking motion. Larger pieces with more layers will take longer to felt than smaller pieces, so will require more rolling. I prefer to roll for about forty to sixty rolls at a time and turn my work frequently so I can constantly check my progress. This is particularly relevant when working with a resist to check that all is in place and no ridges are forming around the edges of your work. You need to understand what you are doing too and why you are doing it, so you know when to move onto the next stage. I will keep on working with the noodle until I see the wool is really tight to the edge of the resist and any decoration I have applied is in place and not moving. I will roll without the noodle until the fibres are no longer lifting and the piece is showing definite signs of shrinking. As you progress through the rolling process, you can slowly increase the pressure. If you start to full your felt too soon, before all the fibres have meshed all the way through all the layers, you will only felt the outer surface of your piece and not the centre and it will not make a stable, strong and hard-wearing felt.

FULLING

It is tempting to skip this final stage of felting or start to full too early, so it is important to observe how your wool fibres are behaving throughout the feltmaking process. Fulling is the final stage where you are shrinking the wool to make a compact, tight fabric. This is achieved through applying heat and friction. I heat my work by placing it in a bowl in a microwave and heat in thirty second bursts, turning the work so it heats evenly. Start gently, warm the work until it is hand-hot and roll, then throw and massage until it is cool. With subsequent heating, you can increase the temperature until the final fulling when it is too hot to hold, either rolling in a mat or towel, or using rubber gloves until it is cool enough to handle. Always ensure that your work is wet before placing in the microwave. By using this method, I find the whole piece is warmed through. However, you may not have a microwave or prefer not to warm your work in this way. You can heat up your work by squeezing out the cold water and plunging it

into a bowl of hot water or pouring hot water over your piece. Have a sponge handy to mop up the excess water, as you will use more with this method, and be careful not to scald yourself. For smaller pieces, the heat of your hands can be enough to felt your work by rubbing and rolling vigorously, using plenty of soap in order not to lift the fibres. The felt is fulled properly if you cannot feel any movement in the fibres when you squeeze the work between your fingers.

WORKING WITH BATTS

I frequently work with Bergschaf batts. With practice, you can split and lay out the batts in one layer but, unless you are very familiar with the wool you are working with, it is very tricky to lay the batts down evenly, especially if they have been folded in storage. When working on a large scale, you can lay down batts very quickly; on a small scale, when using resists, it is much easier to lay down in the same way as roving. Shake out your batt and pull out into a flat sheet, then divide it by gently splitting it into thin, even layers. When holding the batt, try not to scrunch it in your hand to prevent clumpy shingles. Pull off the shingles in the same manner as roving.

Bergschaf and many natural wools take much more wetting down than softer fibres. They also spread considerably once wet. Once the first two layers are wetted down, lay subsequent layers 1cm (0.5in) inside the outer edge, otherwise your work will expand and be larger than your template. Continue to add further layers of wool fibre and repeat from Step 8 in the roving sample instructions.

PROJECT ▶ MAKING A SQUARE SAMPLE USING BATTS

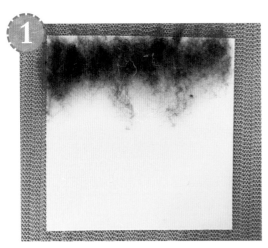

As the staple is often shorter in batts, you may need to lay down more rows.

As the wool tends to spread when wet, take care to keep the fibres within your square.

Lay the second layer at right angles to the first. If there appear to be any thinner sections, it is easy to 'patch' with small pieces of wool to even out.

Take care when wetting down not to spread the fibres too far beyond your template.

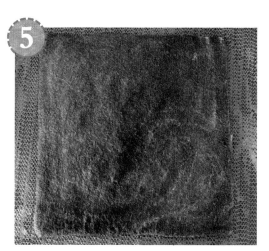

Ensure that the fibres are thoroughly wet before starting to roll. This may entail massaging with soapy hands.

USING A RESIST

When using a resist, you are creating a seamless, three-dimensional piece of felt by covering both sides of the resist with wool fibres. This technique can be tricky at the beginning as it is difficult to reconcile the finished result with the starting point. It is important to walk before you run, so make sure you have made plenty of flat felt samples, and understand the feltmaking process, before tackling working with a resist. Start by making a small, simple case first so you can get to grips with the technique before you progress to more complex designs.

WETTING DOWN

Certain wools with more lanolin or harder scales may be more resistant to wetting down. To encourage water to penetrate through the fibres, lay a piece of bubble wrap with the bubble side face down over the work and massage with soapy hands for a few minutes. Then remove the bubble wrap and gently rub the fibres directly with your hands using extra soap and warm water. Another method is to lay a sheet of netting (tulle) over the work, dab with soap and rub gently with your hands, a scrunched-up plastic bag or a suitable felting tool. Be careful not to felt the fibres to the netting by pulling the fibres through the holes. Get into the habit of wetting down two layers of wool at a time. Less water will be required to wet down the upper layers, as the water from the underneath layers will penetrate through the top layers. It makes it simpler to keep track of the number of layers and prevents the wool from 'growing' as you add more layers.

It is important to ensure that the fibres are fully wet and not fluffy before you start to roll. If, during rolling, you notice that the fibres do appear fluffy, then you need to repeat the process described above.

PROJECT ▶ GLASSES/PHONE/SCISSORS CASE

By changing the scale and shape of the resist, you can create cases to hold a variety of items.

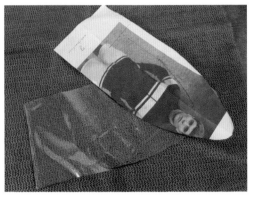

It is sensible to draft your resist on newspaper (folded in half so you can make your design symmetrical) and make any necessary adjustments before cutting out your resist.

The following instructions are for a scissors case but can easily be adapted to make a glasses or phone case. How to calculate the size of your resist to ensure your case is the correct size will be explained in a later chapter. If you have not used a resist before then consider starting with a rectangular resist 35cm × 15cm (6in × 14in) to make a glasses case. Round the corners of the plastic resist so they do not pierce through your wool fibres. Use two colours of wool. You will achieve an interesting blend with a different coloured cuff, and it makes it easier to remember how many layers you have laid down. This is especially relevant as you need to match each side identically. It also illustrates how the fibres migrate through the felt surface to produce a rich, tweed effect. Have fun experimenting with different colour combinations. I have used Corriedale wool for this project.

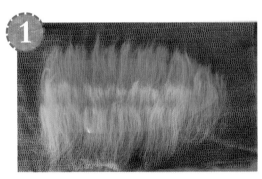

Place your plastic resist on your non-slip mat or bubble wrap. Lay rows of shingles on the resist in your first layer (inside of case), extending beyond the resist edge by 2.5cm (1in).

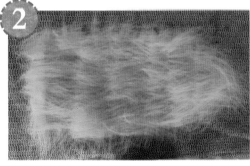

Lay a second layer of shingles at 90 degrees to the first layer.

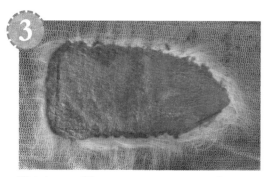

Wet down with warm, soapy water, trying to keep the overlapping edges dry. Cover with bubble wrap and gently rub. Cover with the mat or bubble wrap and turn the work over.

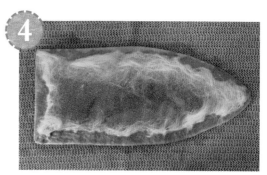

Carefully fold the overlapping fibres over the edge of the resist, easing them to avoid any folds or creases.

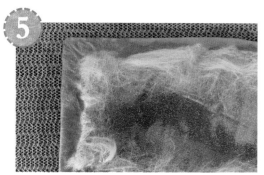

Take extra care folding in the corners, pulling off any excess fibres; it is much easier to keep the fibres even when they are dry. Be very gentle and do not pull or drag the fibres.

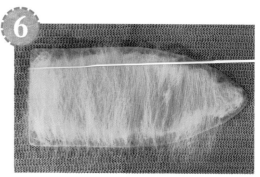

Fill in with a layer of shingles, matching up to the wet edges. You do not need to create a fringe beyond the edge of the resist this time.

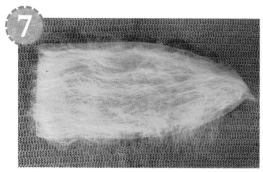

Lay a second layer of shingles at right angles to the first layer.

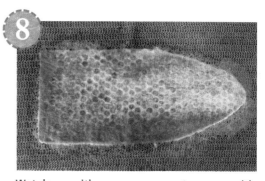

Wet down with warm, soapy water, cover with bubble wrap and gently rub. Do not push the fibres away from the resist edge.

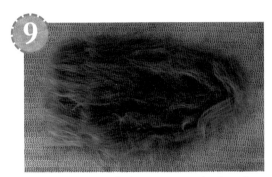

Repeat steps 1 and 2 in your second colour for layers 3 and 4.

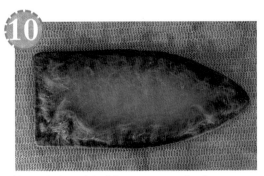

Repeat steps 4 to 8 in your second colour, which will be the outside of the case.

Cover with bubble wrap, bubble side down, and with wet, soapy hands, rub gently, working from the edges in, keeping the fibres tight up to the edge of the resist.

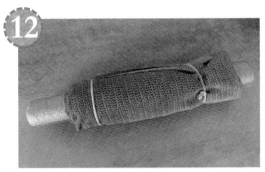

Roll your work fifty times in four directions (as explained in the sample instructions), turn over and repeat. You might find it helpful to tie up the roll to prevent it unwinding.

Your case may be starting to shrink now. If any corners of the resist are poking through your wool, gently ease the resist away by pushing it to the centre of the case. Check that the fibres are stable and not moving, then continue to roll in the mat without the noodle. (If not, roll a little more with the noodle).

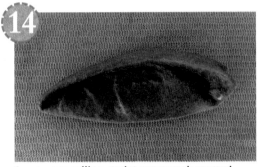

As you are rolling, twist your work around, pushing the resist into the centre away from the edges, working on the seams, rubbing with soapy hands to smooth, so as not to create any ridges.

Keep rolling until the fibres are no longer moving and do not lift when rubbed. You are now ready to warm up the work and start fulling as described in the sample instructions. The resist will scrunch up inside your case.

Pull the case into shape, then cut across the top and remove the resist. Continue to full the piece until it will no longer shrink.

Sometimes edges need a little further work to neaten. Rub them with soap, wrap with a small piece of bubble wrap and rub. A small piece of sponge can also help to hold the bubble wrap while you rub. Fold back the cuff of your case and roll once more so it stays in place, then rinse out well making sure that no soap remains. Reshape the case, rub with a clean piece of bubble wrap or plastic to smooth the surface and leave to dry.

RIDGES

When working with a resist, it is important to avoid forming ridges at the edges. This can occur if: a) you start rolling before you have massaged the edges, so they are tight up to the edge of the resist; or b) you roll for too long without moving your work around the resist. Once you have reached the stage when your work is beginning to shrink and the fibres are stable and no longer moving when you rub the surface, you can start to ease your piece around the resist so you can roll out any ridges. If you are using a plastic resist, warming the work can soften it so you can push it away from the edges. If a ridge has already started to form, stretch it and rub well with soapy hands to remove it. Do keep rotating your work, moving it frequently around the resist and avoid rolling for too long in any one direction.

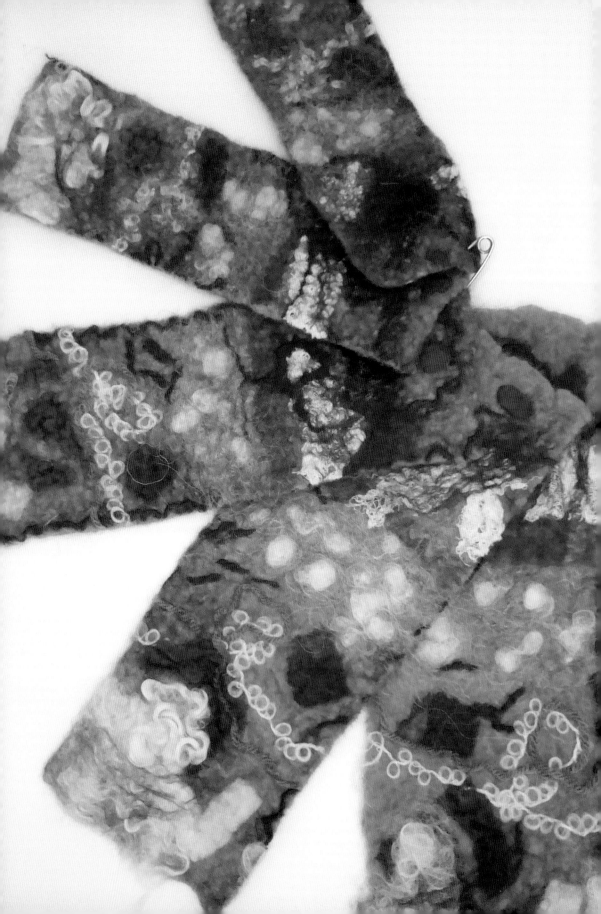

DECORATION

There are infinite ways of applying surface decoration to felt and too many to describe in this book. Decoration is a very personal choice. We all have individual preferences – you will develop your own style over time. Much can be achieved by simply playing with colour without the addition of extra texture. The projects in this book show various methods of decoration. Use these as inspiration to experiment and discover your own style. It is important to focus on the form and function of your bag initially then to decorate your bag with a sympathetic design to complement its form. Often simple is best.

CHOICE OF DECORATION

You can use most natural yarns and fibres to create pattern and texture; although many will not felt by themselves, they will combine with the wool fibres. Even some synthetic fibres will felt in with the wool but take more time to work in. It is wise to avoid these initially.

The following can all be used as surface decoration for felt.

Wool yarns and threads

There are some beautiful varieties on the market, from space dyed to bouclé, and mixtures too such as cashmere, bamboo, mohair. The list is endless. They are a simple and effective way of adding pattern, colour and texture to your work. I have a large stash that I have collected over the years; odd balls left over from crochet and knitting projects or found in charity shops. Yarns with a looser twist felt in better than those with a tighter one and definitely avoid any that are machine washable such as 'Superwash', as these have been treated to prevent shrinkage and will not felt.

Silk threads and fibres

There are many products sold specifically for feltmaking such as silk hankies and silk paper. These work well for making garments but, as a felt bag needs to be well felted, they might be absorbed too much by the wool to have a noticeable effect.

There is also an abundance of other fibres which felt with wool such as flax, bamboo, soya, viscose and alpaca. They can add texture and sheen but may not be as hard-wearing as

Left: Making a set of surface decoration samples is a beneficial exercise to help understand the stages of the felting process.

wool so choose with care depending on the function of your bag and how much wear and tear it will attract.

Nepps

These are the waste material from spinning yarn, can come in a range of colours and are excellent for adding spots of colour.

Raw fleece

This can add wonderful texture to your work when applied to the surface of carded wool. The effect will vary according the breed of wool used and the thickness and quantity applied to the surface.

Pre-felts

Pre-felt is a term that is given to the first stage of the feltmaking process before the work is fulled. It can refer to a) felt that has just been rolled lightly with a noodle so the fibres are still loose and fluffy or b) a very firm piece that is ready to be fulled. Experiment with pre-felts of varying thickness and firmness for creating patterns that need strong outlines and definition. Firmer pre-felts will give a more defined outline but take more effort to felt in to the surface, whilst softer ones will be easier to felt in but will not leave such a clear shape. Over time, you will build up a stash of pre-felts to incorporate into your designs. Pre-felts are often confused with needlefelt, which is produced by machine and is available to buy from various suppliers in a range of colours and thicknesses. They work in a similar way and produce crisp shapes.

SURFACE DECORATION SAMPLES

Experiment with different fibres to see how they felt into the surface before using them on a finished project. When you lay out your design it may well seem well defined and vibrant but when the piece has been completely fulled, the pattern may be totally absorbed by the wool and not as you expect. Generally, the coarser wool varieties absorb

Over time you will build up a collection of pre-felts to use as decoration.

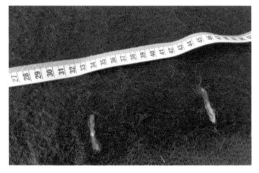

Before you add your decoration, place a marker such as a short piece of wool yarn at regular intervals along your piece – in this example they were 11cm (4.25in) apart.

decoration more than the finer ones – Gotland soaks up other fibres like a sponge. Make a couple of samples using the following guidelines to help you understand how to control the decoration.

Lay out and wet down four layers of your chosen background wool, approximately 60cm × 30cm (24in × 12in). In this sample I have used Zwartbles and I have not folded over the edges. Always wet the wool before adding your decoration otherwise the wetting-down process will rearrange the decoration.

Lay a selection of fibres and yarns across your sample. From top to bottom I have used:
• Wool yarn
• Bouclé yarn
• Coloured nepps
• Untwisted wool used for knitting and felting
• Softly felted pre-felt triangles with firmer felted strips
• Fancy space dyed wool yarn
• Mohair yarn
• Bamboo fibres
• Fancy slub yarn
• Scoured, uncarded Wensleydale
• Silk yarn
• Firmer pre-felt squares
• Nepps
• Cotton scrim
• Flax fibres

Lay out your chosen decoration across the whole piece.

Smooth the plastic down and remove air bubbles to ensure it stays in place when rolling.

Wet down and cover with a piece of thin plastic dust sheet or equivalent. Spray a little water over the plastic and rub with soapy hands to secure the decoration. Turn your work over and check that the fibres are wet and not fluffy. If you are using a coarser wool such as Zwartbles, you may need to gently rub with soapy hands so that the fibres are wet and ready to start felting. Roll your piece in a mat sixty times in each direction with a noodle, then turn over and repeat. Check that the wool fibres are still wet and not fluffy. Give them an extra rub with soapy hands, if not.

After rolling with and without the noodle, the decoration should be firmly in place.

Keeping the thin plastic in place, repeat the rolling without the noodle. Gently lift off the thin plastic – your decoration should now stay in place. If not, replace the plastic and continue rolling until they no longer move.

Cut a strip off your piece using the first marker as a guide and put to one side. Continue to felt the remaining felt by rolling, squeezing and rolling. Once it has shrunk a little more, cut off a further strip and set aside. Continue to felt the work, heating it up and applying more force. Cut off the third strip

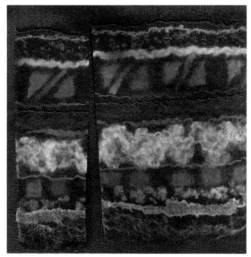

The first segment reveals that the decoration sits on the surface, is not felted in and will easily pull away.

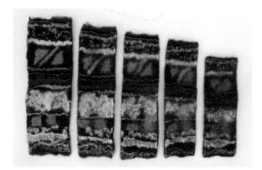

Once completed you can keep your set of samples as a handy reference tool to compare the different stages of felting.

and continue felting; repeat until you have six strips. The final strip should be fully felted and should no longer shrink. Rinse out the strips and leave to dry. You will be surprised by the difference in feel and decoration detail between the first and last strip.

During my feltmaking journey, I have tried out many different methods of surface decoration and now have my personal favourites. You will soon develop a palette of 'additions' that suit your personal taste and identify those that you will never use again! In each bag project in this book, I have shown a different method of decoration to inspire you. You can also achieve much by simply using colour.

PROJECT ▶ SURFACE DECORATION SAMPLES

This is one of the simplest ways to make a bag as it does not require adding a separate handle. You can, therefore, concentrate on exploring surface pattern. The shape can be adapted to make a shopper basket shape or a bucket bag. You can also make more of a feature of the handle by cutting out an oval or a circle rather than a slit, which I have shown here. My pebble collection inspired the decoration of the bag, so I decided to use a pebble shape

An easy project for a beginner made with one basic resist. The shape, decoration and size of the bag can easily be altered.

for the bag too. Designing your bag and calculating shrinkage to work out the size of your resist will be described in Chapter 4. For this example, I used four layers of Zwartbles wool. Refer to Chapter 2 for more detailed instructions on laying down the wool, using a resist and the felting process. You need to decide where you are going to place your handle at this stage as it will affect where you lay out your surface decoration.

As the decoration of this bag is solely on the surface, lay down four layers of wool on each side of the resist as described in Chapter 2.

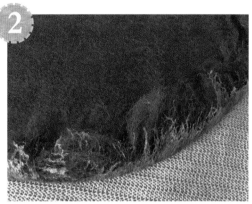

To ensure that the wool is tight against your resist, gently rub your bar of soap along the edge without pulling or dragging the fibres.

To strengthen your handle area, lay down another layer of wool fibres on either side of the resist.

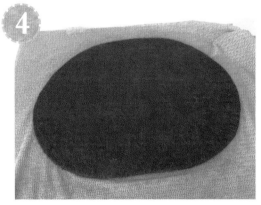

Once all four layers are complete, wetted down and tight against the edge of your resist, you are ready to add the decoration.

Adding the surface decoration

Sketch out your design on paper before you start and prepare the fibres you are using for the decoration. Use a watercolour pencil to mark out some outlines directly onto the bag surface to guide you and also mark where you will place the handle. To recreate the pattern and texture of a pebble, I used a combination of nepps, silk, wool and bouclé yarns, scoured, uncarded Wensleydale wool, fine wool threads and fibres, flax fibres and cotton scrim, all in natural colours.

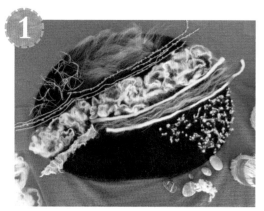

Allow your decoration to continue over the edge so you can easily match it on the other side. Taking a photograph or making a sketch at this point will serve as a reminder.

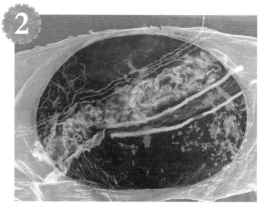

Wet down and cover with thin plastic dust sheet. Sprinkle with water and rub with soapy hands.

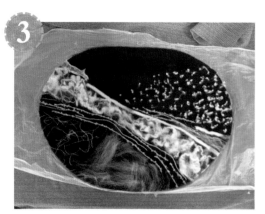

Turn the bag over and match up the decoration, wrapping it around the sides, wet down and cover with thin plastic dust sheet. Sprinkle with water and rub with soapy hands.

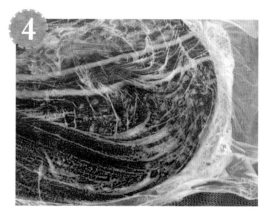

Before you start rolling, making sure you have plenty of soapy water on the plastic, rub well on both sides, pushing in from the sides so the edges are tight to the resist.

Felting the bag

Sandwiching the bag in a non-slip mat, roll your piece sixty times in each direction with a noodle, then turn it over and repeat. At this stage, it is advisable to check how the wool is felting. Your decoration should be staying in place. However, as some wools take more time to absorb water, if the fibres appear fluffy, wet them down a little more with warm water and rub with soapy hands. Replace the thin plastic sheets on both sides, roll sixty times in each direction without the noodle, turn over and repeat. By this stage, you should see some shrinkage with the wool fibres pulling against the resist. If you have not quite reached this stage, do some further rolling.

Ease the edges of the bag away from the resist and push it into the centre of the bag so the fibres can shrink and are not stretched by the resist.

Continue to roll, turning the work regularly and pushing the bag around the resist to avoid ridges forming.

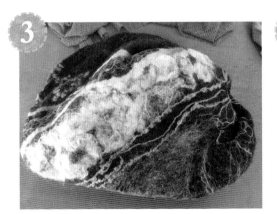

Apply soap to the bag to prevent the fibres from lifting, scrunch, throw and roll to further felt and shrink. Warm the work and start to full.

Continue to shrink the bag until it is almost fully felted. Pull it into shape with the resist pushed into the centre. You can check the size with the original paper template.

Cutting the handle

Fold the bag in half widthways and, with a watercolour pencil, mark the halfway point at the top of the bag where you will cut the bag opening. Then measure down equally on either side, usually about two thirds up from the bottom. How large you make the opening depends on the design of your bag: too large, and the contents will fall out; too small, and it will be difficult to retrieve the contents. This example has a 30cm (12in) opening, 15cm (12in) either side of the halfway mark. Neatly cut the top open with sharp scissors.

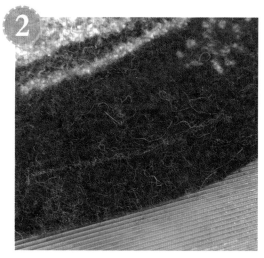

Remove the resist and decide where you would like to place the handle. This could be a straight line, an oval or a circle depending on the design of your bag. It is important that you do not make the handle too thin, otherwise it will be too weak and stretch.

FINISHING EDGES

For a professional finish, it is important to have sealed and neat edges on your work and there are varying methods of achieving this. Wet felt stretches very easily so care must be taken not to distort the edge and pull it out of shape, especially if you cut your project when it is only very lightly felted. For this reason, I recommend leaving cutting open your bag to remove the resist for as long as possible. Later in the book, I explain how to avoid unnecessary stretching by stitching the edges. You can neaten edges by rubbing with plenty of soap, using either bubble wrap or a felting tool. Care needs to be taken to rub evenly and not to pull the edge out of shape. However, rolling will often give a better finish; just work on the edge and not the whole bag. Heating the felt and using a piece of wooden doweling to roll, so you can really apply pressure, is very effective. Rolling with soapy hands can pull in an edge too. Each wool breed behaves differently, those with a shorter staple tend to form a neater edge.

In this example, the handle is 4cm (2.75in) wide and 16cm (6.5in) long. Mark with a watercolour pencil before you cut. You can easily rub out the pencil marks but you cannot repair a cut in the wrong place. Cut on one side first, then turn over and match the cut on the reverse.

Final fulling and finishing

Warm up the bag (you can make it very hot at this stage), roll, scrunch and throw, remembering to add soap so as not to lift the fibres. Reheat, if necessary, and continue to full the bag until the edges are sealed and it will shrink no further. As the edges of the bag were cut when the fibres were almost fully felted, they should firm up with the rolling and not require working by hand.

Rinse out all the soap – you can spin dry your bag after rinsing. If you do not have access to a spin dryer, you can roll the rinsed bag in a clean, dry towel to remove excess water. At this stage, pull and stretch the bag into shape, pushing with your fists or shape around wooden tools or plastic bowls; anything that comes to hand which is the right shape. Fully felted, wet wool is incredibly strong and you can apply real force to manipulate it into shape. You can also stuff the bag with newspaper, a towel or bubble wrap. Give the bag a rub over with a plastic bag, metal spoon or pebble to flatten down any loose hairs. Leave to dry, tweaking the shape as necessary. Once dry, you can iron the bag to further smooth any loose hairs.

USING A SPIN DRYER

A spin dryer is most useful for removing excess water as it is astonishing how much water felt retains. Large, thick felt takes some time to dry. The weight of the water can also make it tricky to shape your work. Take care in spinning unfinished items as the friction continues to felt the wool and may be undesirable if you are drying pre-felts. For this reason, try to avoid using modern washing machines that only have a long rinse and spin option, which can over-felt and distort your work. With a free-standing spin dryer, you can control the length of the spin – thirty seconds to a minute is often perfectly adequate.

DESIGNING YOUR BAG

Having trained as a designer, I consider it vital that you understand the materials you are working with – then you are in control rather than the materials controlling you. Your choice of materials, colour and decoration will define the character of your bag.

FUNCTION AND FORM

Design is simply puzzle solving. Write a brief first then you will not begin with a blank piece of paper. You will need to ask several questions and the answers will form the basis of your design.

Why are you making the bag – what is its purpose?

Before you even start sketching out your design, write a list describing the purpose of the bag you wish to make. As the felting process is labour intensive, this saves time and will help you design a practical and functional bag.

What will the bag hold?

The purpose of your bag will determine how you approach the design and execution. Guessing the size, especially if the bag will contain a specific item such as a computer, is not good practice. If you have to stop felting your bag because it is becoming too small, the wool fibres will not have fully felted and your bag will not wear well, as it will become fluffy and pill. It is essential to make a square sample in your chosen wool as described in Chapter 2 to calculate the shrinkage to ensure that your bag will be the correct size. The end purpose of your bag will also affect your choice of wool and the number of layers required. To add extra protection for a delicate item such as a pair of glasses, a phone or computer, you might consider using a stronger wool, maybe Bergschaf or Finn wool with more layers. This reasoning also applies if you are making a larger bag that will hold heavy items. For a decorative bag that will only be used occasionally, you might choose a softer wool such as merino or blue-faced Leicester.

How often will you use your bag?

A handbag that is used every day will endure

Left: It is important to design and select your materials before you start to make your bag.

much more wear and tear than a clutch bag that is only used occasionally and does not attract heavy handling. This will also affect your choice of wool, decoration and the number of layers of wool.

How will you carry your bag?

Some bags may not require handles, such as clutch bags and cases for phones and glasses. However, most will need a handle of some sort. Chapter 5 will look at handles in depth, but you need to decide on your form of handle before you start. It is vital to consider the length, the strength and the number of handles depending on the function and scale of your bag.

How will you make your bag secure?

Depending on the function of your bag, the security of its contents needs consideration, as it will affect the final look and function of your bag. I have seen some stunning felt bags that are not at all practical. Is the flap large enough to fold over the opening? What kind of fastening does the bag need? Will everything fall out if it is turned upside down or be an open invitation to a pickpocket?

How will your bag be used?

Give some thought as to how your bag will be used. You will need to allow extra room for ease of access – you will struggle to remove a phone from its case if it is too tight a fit. It is harder to find items in a deep bag so perhaps increase the width rather than the depth. Is it desirable to have some pockets on either the inside or the outside of the bag for smaller items?

Once you have worked your way through all the questions, you will have set some limitations which will help you create your design. Start off with some quick sketches to work out the size and shape of your bag, the style and position of handle and fastening, and the placement of any pockets. Deciding on all these elements in advance makes it easier to map out your bag form, which you can further develop into an attractive and pleasing design. Ensure that the look of the bag suits the function. The next project talks you through the design stages and will give you a better understanding of the process.

PROJECT ▶ CLUTCH BAG WITH BUTTON FASTENING

The decoration and choice of button can transform a simple design.

For this project, I have chosen a rectangular shape, with no handles but have included a pocket as an extra challenge. This format can easily be adapted to make a clutch bag, a purse, or a case for jewellery or a notepad. This design is a case for my rotary cutter and blades in order to keep them together, as the two never seem to be in the same place. I have used merino wool, one colour for the first two layers with a mix of colours for the final two layers. Please refer to the earlier chapters for full descriptions of the felting process where appropriate. Whenever I refer to two layers, they are placed at right angles to each other. Make notes of your progress to keep track of the number of layers you have laid down and take photographs too so you can check that the decoration matches on both sides of your bag.

Calculating the enlargement/ shrinkage factor

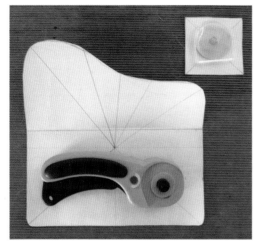

It is vitally important to draft out your design. It is far better to have a bag that is slightly big rather than too small for its intended purpose.

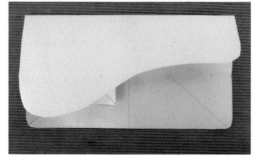

Ensure that the flap is large enough so that the bag's contents do not fall out.

To make a case or bag to fit a specific item such as a phone, you will need to draw around it first. Then add at least 2–3cm (1in) all the way round to allow for a gusset, taking into account the depth of the item plus extra to prevent too tight a fit. Now you can play with the shape for the bag and flap. Do the same for the pocket and plan the placement of this so it is accessible.

Although this may seem like a chore, making samples so you can calculate shrinkage does save you time in the long run. Bit by bit, you will build up a series of samples in different wool breeds in various thicknesses so you can refer to these rather than making fresh samples. Remember to label your samples with wool type, number of layers and weight of the fibres. You may like to note the supplier too, as fibres can vary. If you always start with a 20cm (8in) square, it makes it straightforward when calculating the enlargement/shrinkage factor. When I first started making felt, I was too enthusiastic and made random-sized samples and did not take notes. These pieces are useful to use as coasters but not helpful for either calculating the enlargement/shrinkage factor or repeating the original effect.

The enlargement/shrinkage factor is calculated by dividing the original square sample size before felting by the final size when fully felted and dry. For this example, I used four layers of merino wool fibres. My finished sample measures 11cm × 11cm (4.4in × 4.25in). Therefore, if I divide the original 20cm (8in) by 11cm (4.4in), I will arrive at the enlargement/shrinkage factor of 1.818. This can be rounded up to 1.82 to simplify the calculations. Make a note of this factor as you will now use it to calculate the size of your resist. For those with a mathematical mind, you can also work out the shrinkage as a percentage. However, this can be confusing, as the shrinkage percentage differs from the enlargement percentage.

Before you start, prepare your equipment; you will need a ruler, calculator, paper, scissors and pencil. I find newspaper ideal for making templates. Do make paper templates before transferring to your resist material as it is easy to make mistakes in your calculations.

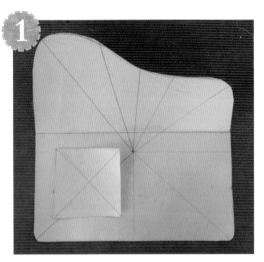

To work out the correct size of your resist template, first make a paper template for the actual size of your bag design (including the flap and pocket). Mark the centre of your design and draw lines through key points on the bag. Lay this paper template in the centre of a larger piece of paper.

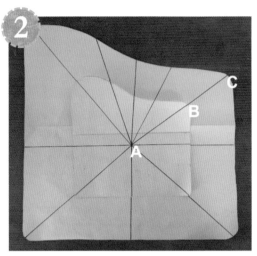

Measure from the centre of the bag template (point A) to one of the key points on the edge (point B). Multiply this by the enlargement/shrinkage factor, so AC = AB × 1.82. Repeat this on the key points to create an outline for the resist template.

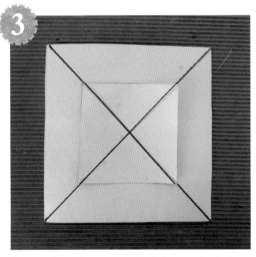

Repeat the enlargement/shrinkage calculations for the pocket and cut out the paper templates. It is useful to keep these for future projects to either repeat or adapt the design.

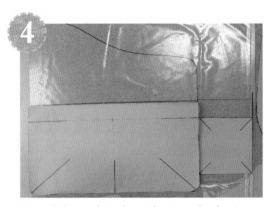

Extend the pocket along the top edge by 3cm (1.2in) and mark a line along the original pocket top. Using the paper templates, cut out your resists, marking a line where the flap folds over with a permanent marker and round off any sharp corners.

Making a pocket

Set up to felt with your chosen wool and decoration for the project. The pocket is prepared first. Note: it is very easy to forget this stage and start laying down the wool on the bag resist.

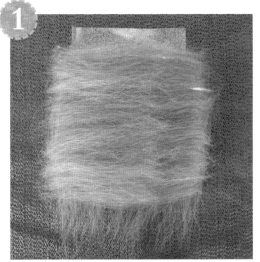

Lay down two layers of wool up to the marked line and extending over the three other edges by 1.5cm (0.6in). Wet down, keeping the edges dry, then turn over.

Fold the fibres over, ensuring that they are tight to the edge of the resist, easing out any creases. Turn over and lay down a further two layers.

After wetting down and folding over the fibres on the reverse of the resist, fold over the fibres at the top of the pocket to the marked line to form a neat edge.

Position the pocket on the main bag resist as shown, with the folded edges uppermost, making sure that it is in the correct position, not too close to the top of the flap or the edge of the bag.

Making the bag

Lay a row of shingles along the edge of the flap of your bag, with the 'head' of the shingle to the centre and the 'tail' to the outside, in the colour that will form the inside of the bag.

Continue to lay two layers of wool over the resist. Wet down, keeping the edges dry, then turn over.

Fold the loose fibres over, ensuring that they are tight to the edge of the resist, easing out any creases. Lay a strip of thin plastic along the line where the flap will fold.

Lay down two layers of wool meeting the folded-over edges from the back and extending slightly over the marked fold line. Wet down.

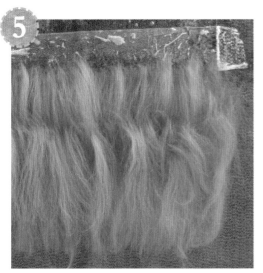

Lay down two layers of wool in the colour(s) that will be the outside of the bag. As this is a small bag, I kept the decoration simple and used colour to create the pattern. This shows the first layer using two shades of blue. To achieve this effect, split the roving into two thinner ropes and hold both colours in your hand as you pull off the shingles. The colours will mix in a random fashion for an abstract effect.

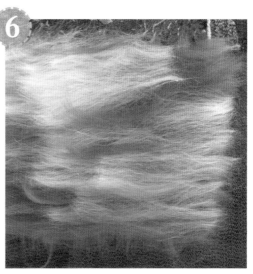

Lay down the second layer of wool using the same technique and different colours. The colours will all blend when felted. Wet down.

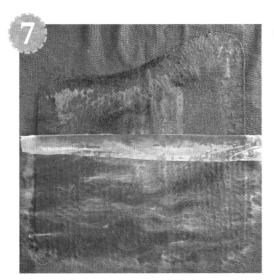

Fold over the edge along the marked line using the thin plastic to create a neat edge. Turn over.

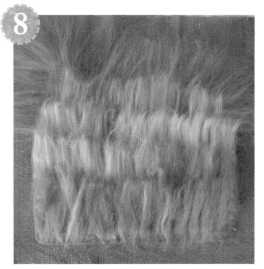

Fold over the edges as described previously. Creating a fringe around the flap edge as before, lay down the third layer of wool meeting the folded edges.

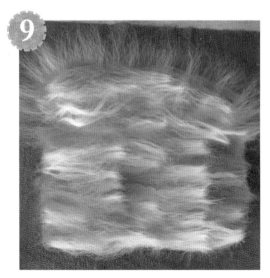

Repeat with the fourth layer, wet down and turn over. Fold over the edges on the flap, easing out any creases.

Gently place a small strip of thin plastic at the edge of the flap fold between the resist and front of the bag on each side to prevent it felting to the flap.

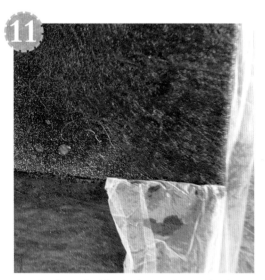

Ease it down inside the bag so it remains in place when rolling. Turn over.

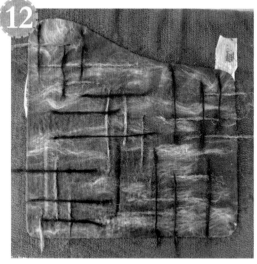

Add any further decoration. I used a mixture of yarn and pencil roving to create a 1950s style pattern. Remember to continue your pattern around the edges and that the flap will be the dominant feature of the bag. Wet down and cover with thin plastic.

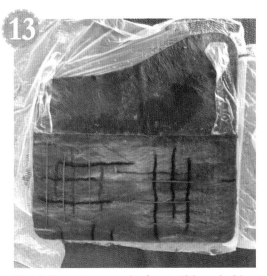

Match the pattern on the front. Although this will be covered by the flap, it will be seen when the bag is open. Wet down and cover with thin plastic.

Removing the flap resist and felting the bag

Felting the bag

Before you start rolling, make sure you have plenty of soapy water on the plastic. Massage well on both sides, working on the edges so they are tight to the resist. Sandwiching the bag in a non-slip mat, roll your piece fifty times in each direction with a noodle. Turn over and repeat. At this stage, it is advisable to check how the wool is felting. If your decoration is not staying in place, wet down with warm water and rub gently with soapy hands. Roll a little more until the decoration is no longer moving and the bag is starting to shrink. Do not move on to the next stage until you have reached this point.

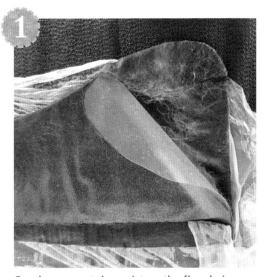

Gently ease out the resist on the flap, being careful not to stretch the fibres.

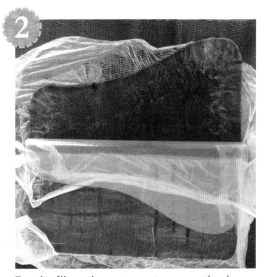

Tap the fibres down to create a smooth edge on the flap.

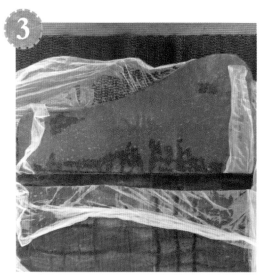

Fold the resist back over the top of the flap. Replace the thin plastic sheets on both sides between the flap and front of the bag, and roll fifty times in each direction without the noodle.

By this stage, you should see some shrinkage with the wool pulling against the resist. Fold in the sides of the resist plastic to prevent the fibres being stretched, not forgetting to do the same with the pocket resist. Turn the work over and continue to roll until the fibres no longer move.

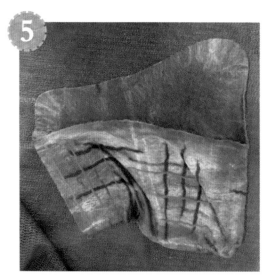

Carefully remove the resist and gently rub the edges with soapy hands to smooth out any ridges.

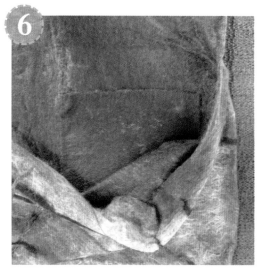

The pocket should be firmly felted in place. Remove the pocket resist plastic and gently rub some soap on the inside to prevent it from sticking to the back of the bag.

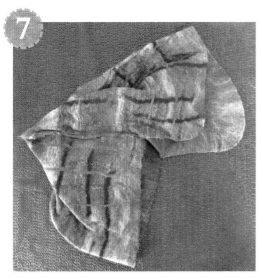

Continue to roll, turning the work regularly to avoid ridges forming. Apply soap to the bag to prevent the fibres from lifting. Scrunch, throw and roll to further felt and shrink. Heating the work at this stage will speed up the process.

If the bag opening is stretching too much, sew a running stitch along the edge with strong thread doubled up.

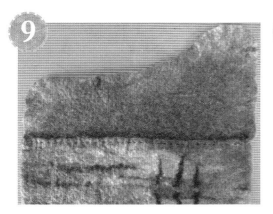

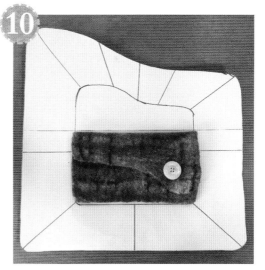

Pull the thread tight so that the edge is the correct length and firmly fasten off the ends. The thread can be removed once the bag is finished and dry if it is still visible.

Continue to shrink the bag until it is almost fully felted. You can check the shrinkage rate against your original design. You may need to roll more in one direction to obtain the correct proportions.

Cutting a buttonhole

If you cut your buttonhole too soon, it may stretch and become too large. Plan the position of the button and mark the length with a watercolour pencil.

Cut the buttonhole shorter than the marked length as it will stretch slightly. Rub with soapy fingers then heat and roll to seal the edges. Continue fulling the bag until it has shrunk down to the size of the original design template.

Rinse out the bag thoroughly to remove all traces of soap. Shape the bag by stretching with your hands or using wooden or plastic formers. Rub the surface with plastic or a spoon to smooth and polish the surface. You can stuff with newspapers or bubble wrap to keep the shape whilst it is drying. Once dry, iron the bag to remove any hairiness and sew on the button.

A FEW EXTRA TIPS

- You do not have to complete your project all in one go – I often lay down the wool, wet it down, leave it to rest and start the felting later. This 'resting' time allows the scales to fully open up, speeding up the felting. Do not roll up your work, but rather leave it flat as the water will pool to the lowest point. If you have the space to be able to leave your work and return to it later, it is worth developing this habit as it will also give your back a rest.

- I sometimes run out of time to complete a project in a single felting session. I will work the piece to a firm pre-felt stage before leaving to complete later. You do not need to rinse out the soap, just gently squeeze out the excess water and leave to dry flat. If you are just leaving the work for a few days, wrap it up in bubble wrap or in a towel.

- If you do leave your wet work for some time, sprinkle with warm water to warm it up.

- Remember that you can continue felting your work at any time, even after it has been finished and rinsed. Simply wet it down with hot, soapy water and continue to full the piece. You will be surprised how much firmer it will become – and quickly too.

- After rinsing out all the soap from your work, you can still heat it up by plunging it in hot water, microwaving it or steaming it to pull it into shape. Hot felt is much more elastic than cold felt.

- To remove excess fibre and guard hairs, rub over the wet surface with your hand or a plastic bag.

- It is best to shave off surplus hair when your work is dry.

- Experiment with the way you work, perhaps use a broom handle or plastic piping instead of a soft noodle to help your rolling action. Each feltmaker applies different pressure when rolling so you may need to adapt your technique.

- When you reach the fulling stage, try rolling your work in a wet towel or cotton sheeting.

- Each feltmaker develops their own technique, so experiment to discover what works best for you. It does not matter what methods you use, as long as you end up with a properly fully-felted end result.

- There is always something new to discover about wool and the felting process. Never stop practising and learning.

HANDLES AND FASTENINGS

Imagine a teapot without a handle and with a spout that drips. Unthinkable. Equally, the handle is one of the most important elements of your bag and will take the most wear and tear with constant handling: you want it to be attractive but also functional. This is also true of the method you choose to fasten the bag, and this will affect the design and position of your flap.

Never start making a bag before you have decided the design and placement of the handles, fastenings and pockets. The thrill of making three-dimensional felt using a resist can often mean that these are considered as an afterthought. They need to be prepared in advance of laying down the main section of the bag and can be awkward to add later if you forget to do this. They are crucial elements of creating a functional bag. Instructions on how to attach handles and fastenings are explained in the projects in Chapters 6 and 7.

HANDLES

I enjoy the challenge of solving the design problem to create handles that both complement the bag and are functional. Two options with variations are described in detail in the projects in Chapters 6 and 7; integral handles that are part of the bag's resist and added handles which are created separately.

Handles do not necessarily have to be made from felt; a range of leather, wood and plastic handles can be bought ready-made. If you choose to use these, do ensure that they suit the design and function of your bag and do not appear as if they are an afterthought.

Deciding on the size and function of your bag will determine the type of handles required. Consider the following.

Length of handle

Are you making a shoulder bag, cross shoulder bag or one that rests over your arm? Check the length of your handle before you start and consider the shrinkage ratio. A flat handle will shrink more than a cord handle.

Strength of handle

How much weight will the bag carry? If the bag will hold heavy items, then the handle may stretch, so do ensure that a strong wool is used, well felted with an adequate number of layers of wool.

Left: Simply changing the colour of wool and decoration can change the character of your bag.

Width of handle

How wide or thick does your handle need to be? Too thin a handle will stretch if used as a shoulder bag; however, thick handles may be hard to hold on a shopping bag.

How many handles?

Does your bag need one or two handles? Most bags only require one handle, but shopping bags or baskets may require two.

Position of handle

Where will you place the handles? The position of the handles will determine how the bag hangs and sits when worn. If the handles are too low, the bag may tip over. If they are too far apart, the flap or opening may bulge. You might consider making the handles thicker where they join the bag for extra strength.

PROJECT ▶ MAKING A CORD HANDLE

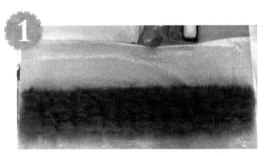

Lay down the first layer of three rows of shingles (on bubble wrap, bubble side down), then a second layer at right angles, a little longer than the desired length of cord.

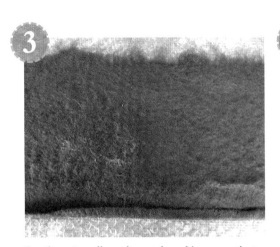

Wet down. Fold up 1cm (0.4in) on the bottom edge of the cord.

Continue to roll up the cord, making sure that it is even, and trying to trap as little air as possible.

Working along the entire length, continue to roll up like a Swiss roll, keeping it round rather than flat, without creating any creases.

Cords are very useful for both handles and fastenings; the thickness and length can easily be adjusted to suit your design. The following step-by-step instructions explain how to make a separate cord handle with a starting length of 100cm (40in). If the handle needs to be attached and part of the bag, leave each end dry. This is explained more fully in the Shopper Bag project in Chapter 7. Cords do not shrink dramatically in length, although you can vary their thickness by altering the number of layers and rows of shingles laid down.

Take your time and do not rush, keeping the cord round and even.

Slowly roll the cord by folding over the bubble wrap without flattening it, working up and down the length.

If the ends are too thin, add a little soap and fold up the end.

Continue to roll, either working directly on a rubber mat or in a bamboo mat, with gentle pressure to start, increasing as the cord becomes firmer.

Once the cord is firm and even, warm it up, throw and roll, using plenty of soap so as not to lift the fibres. Repeat this until the cord is very firm as it will become fluffy quickly if it is not fulled sufficiently.

PROJECT ▶ MAKING A FLAT HANDLE

Flat handles are strong and ideal for larger bags, as they sit more comfortably on the shoulder. Start with a length of bubble wrap that is longer than required. In this instance, I laid down a 125cm (50in) length of wool aiming for a finished handle 100cm long (40in) and 4cm (1.6in) wide using two colours for a rich, tweed effect.

Working with the bubble side down (using the flat top surface gives a smoother fold), mark four lines 8cm (3.2in) apart with a permanent marker.

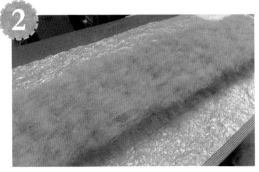

Between the lines, lay down two layers of wool at right angles, with the second layer slightly inside the first.

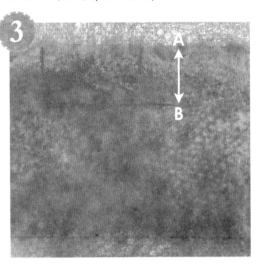

Wet down, keeping both ends dry, and mark the first fold line with a watercolour pencil, AB = 8cm (3.2in).

Carefully fold along the line and press down; lift up the bubble wrap carefully without lifting the fibres.

Repeat the fold on the bottom edge. You should now have six layers folded together, 8cm (3.2in) wide. Tuck in any stray fibres.

Felting the handle

Cover the handle with bubble wrap and massage well, then rub with soapy hands, keeping both ends dry. Work on both sides until the fibres are stable and no longer lift or move. It is important that you reach this point before moving on to the next stage. If the handle is very wet, gently remove any excess water with a sponge (lay some netting or a non-slip mat over the work to prevent the fibres from lifting). You now need to felt the handle by throwing, as rolling can distort it and wet the ends. Holding the bubble wrap either side of the handle widthways, lift up 5–10cm (2–4in)

and drop, working up and down the handle. Avoid holding the handle itself as it will stretch. Continue to do this until the handle feels firm and you can move it without stretching – it should take between five and ten minutes of the tossing action. You can now roll it in the bubble wrap from side to side until it feels firm to the touch and the centre fibres are no longer moving. Squeeze out the excess water and set aside ready to add to your bag. There is no need to rinse it out.

Continually check that both ends are dry throughout the felting process as you will use these fibres to attach the handle to the bag.

You can roll the handle once it is firm enough not to stretch and distort.

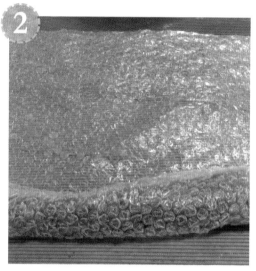

To keep the edges straight, use a length of wooden dowelling and roll on both edges.

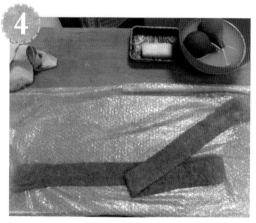

The handle is now ready to attach to the bag with each end dry.

FASTENINGS

How you prevent your bag from falling open and the contents cascading out can be resolved in a number of ways.

Buttons

There is such a wide selection available now in a range of materials and sizes; choose one or two to complement the design of your bag. A button could be the bag's main feature. In Chapter 4, there are instructions on making a buttonhole.

Magnetic clasps

These are available in different sizes and colours, either to sew on or with bend-over tabs. The sew-on variety is preferable, as the tabs need to be concealed either with a folded cuff or a stitched-on detail. They are invaluable when you want a secure, discreet fastening, which does not interfere with the decoration on your bag.

Cord toggles

These are a good solution if you want to make your bag entirely from wool; you can incorporate them into the design of your bag or make them a feature. Variations are described in the projects in Chapter 7.

Flap

If you make a large flap that extends over the opening of the bag, then there may be no need for a fastening, as the weight of the flap will keep the bag closed.

Other suggestions

There are numerous other alternatives, such as zips, poppers and hooks and eyes, although I would avoid Velcro fastenings as they stick to the felt and make it fluffy. You can also buy specialist fittings for clasp purses, buckles, etc. Use this book as a starting point to develop your own methods and techniques.

Sew-on magnet fastenings are an ideal solution for a discreet fastening.

PROJECT ▶ MAKING CORD TOGGLES

This is a basic guide to making cord fastenings; there are specific instructions in the projects in Chapter 7.

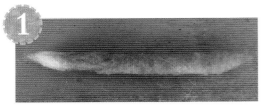

Working on a dry surface (ideally a ribbed rubber mat), lay a length of wool down slightly longer than the final desired length. You can use several colours as desired. Roll dry to eliminate excess air and even out the fibres.

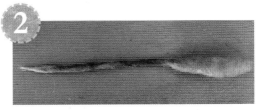

Keeping the end dry, wet down, and gently roll to form a round cord. The wool will stretch and lengthen.

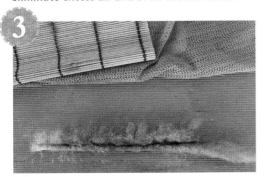

If the cord seems too thin, add extra wool, bearing in mind that it will become smaller when felted.

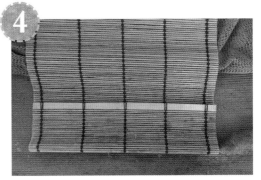

Roll the cord directly on a rubber mat, or roll in bubble wrap or a bamboo mat, remembering to keep the end dry so you can attach it to your bag. Continue to roll until the cord is firm. It does not need to be totally fulled as you will carry on felting it when attached to the bag.

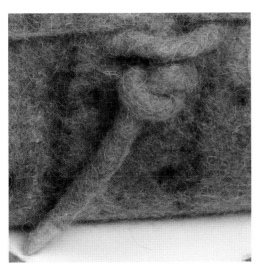

You can experiment with different ways of using cord toggles as fastenings.

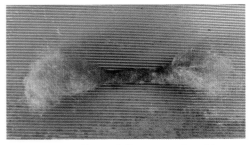

To make a cord loop, follow steps 1 to 4 but keep both ends dry.

BASIC DESIGNS

The projects in this chapter combine various elements to show you different techniques in handles, fastenings and decoration. Refer to the instructions in the previous chapters for more detailed information on the felting process. Once you understand the principles, you can mix and experiment with all the techniques described. Remember to make notes of your progress to keep track of the number of layers you have laid down and take photographs too, so you can check that the decoration matches on both sides of your bag.

PROJECT ▶ OVAL BAG WITH INTEGRAL CORD HANDLE AND STITCHED MAGNETIC FASTENING

The character of the bag can be altered by changing the shape and decoration.

**FABRIC DECORATION
(NUNO, APPLIED OR LAMINATED FELT)**

This is a simple and effective way of creating pattern using up scraps of fabric or charity shop bargains. Natural fabrics, such as silk, cotton, linen and viscose with an open weave, work best as they allow the wool fibres to penetrate through the holes to bond the wool and the fabric together. As the wool fibres shrink, the fabric 'crinkles', giving a wonderful texture. The 'crinkles' will vary in size as more or less wool penetrates through the gaps in the fabric depending on its fineness and thickness. Experiment with different fabrics and wool fibres before embarking on a large project as it is frustrating if you cannot get your fabric to 'felt' in. The trick is to start rolling very gently to ensure the fibres migrate through the fabric. Check they have done so before starting to felt more vigorously or you risk the wool fibres felting separately from the fabric. Throwing the work at the later stages of felting really helps the wool fibres migrate through the fabric. Once your work is finished and dry, you can pull off or shave the excess 'fluff' if it obscures the pattern.

Left: Adding surface decoration can transform a plain shape.

This is an ideal project for a beginner. It is quick to make, as the handle is part of the template, allowing you to explore different methods of decoration. No felt is removed so two flaps are created, one sitting inside the other, forming a secure closure. Use a round resist for your first attempt so you can experiment with the size and shape, decoration and type of wool. Depending on the size and intended use for your bag, you can choose to use either four or six layers of wool. I have used the same template as the bag in Chapter 3 to illustrate how you can create different designs from the same starting point. It is an oval shape, 60cm × 42cm (24in × 16.8in), slightly flatter at the base of the bag with more of a curve at the top, which will form the handle. I have used New Zealand wool, which is similar to merino. The fibres are fine enough to penetrate through the cotton fabric I have incorporated as decoration. I have used the same colour wool throughout to emphasize the brightly patterned fabric.

On both sides in turn, lay bubble wrap over the bag and rub gently, as explained previously, to make sure that the wool is tight up to the edge of the resist. With fabric decoration there is no need to cover with thin plastic but

Lay six layers of your chosen wool on each side of the resist as explained in Chapter 2.

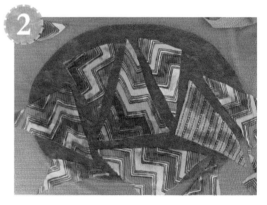

Leaving a 4cm (1.6in) space at the top of your bag (this will be the handle), decorate the bag as you choose.

Remember to 'wrap' your pattern around the bag. To help fold over curved edges, snip the fabric and overlap the edges.

Decorate your bag on both sides, leaving a 4cm (1.6in) space for the handle, which is at the bottom in this image.

HOW LONG TO ROLL?

The amount of rolling varies considerably and depends on a range of factors:

- the size of your work

- the number of layers of wool

- the wool – different breeds felt at different rates

- the type of decoration – some needs more work to felt into the surface

- the temperature – warmth speeds up the felting process

- the method of rolling, as everyone applies different pressure and uses varying motions

Generally, you will need to roll longer for larger and more complex designs. With practice, you will learn how long to spend on each stage of the feltmaking process, which will be personal to you. It is vital to check regularly to see how the work is progressing and when to move on to the next stage.

do use it if you are adding other fibres or yarn decoration. Follow the felting process as described earlier. In this example, I rolled sixty times × 4 on each side, back and front (480 rolls altogether) with the noodle, and the same without the noodle. By this stage, you should clearly see the wool fibres penetrating through the fabric and some shrinkage. You may need to roll more or less to achieve this, depending on your technique.

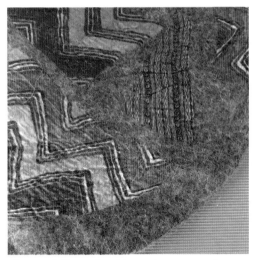

The wool fibres should now be penetrating through the fabric and be clearly visible.

Cutting the handle

Before cutting the handle, ease the plastic resist into the centre of the bag away from the edges. Measure and mark the centre of the bag with a watercolour pencil. Starting approximately one third down, mark a line 3cm (1.2in) in from the edge. With sharp scissors and cutting through the top layer only, carefully cut the marked line.

Wet felt stretches considerably, especially in the pre-felt stage, and it is very easy to pull your work out of shape and distort the edges.

Lay the bag flat and take your time when cutting the handle. It is important to be accurate to make an even cord.

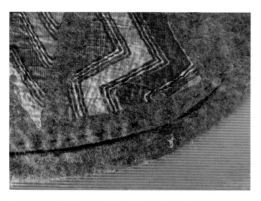

Cut and stitch one side before turning over and repeating on the other side to avoid distorting the shape of your bag.

The stitched flap edges will keep their shape whilst you make the cord handle.

With a strong, synthetic thread, sew a running stitch along the cut edge (not the handle side), securing it well at both ends. If the thread is visible when the bag is complete and dry, it can be removed. Turn the bag over, and repeat the marking, cutting and stitching to match the first side.

Making the cord handle

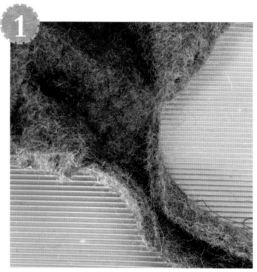

Open out the bag and starting at one end of the handle, open out then fold the edges to meet in the centre.

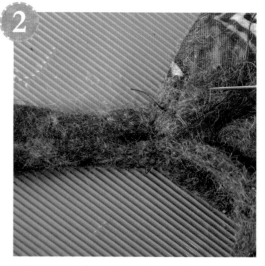

Using strong thread doubled up, fasten securely and pull the edges together tightly.

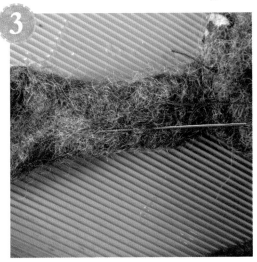

Sew the two sides together using ladder stitch (also known as slip, blind or invisible stitch). Stitching at least 3mm (0.12in) from the edge, a running stitch is sewn on one side.

A running stitch is then sewn on the opposite side. Each stitch should measure approximately 3mm (0.12in).

At regular intervals, pull the thread tight to form an even cord. Continue until you have stitched the length of the handle and fasten securely.

Working on a rubber mat or bubble wrap, rub plenty of soap on your handle. Roll the cord gently at first to prevent creases forming, increasing the pressure as it becomes firmer.

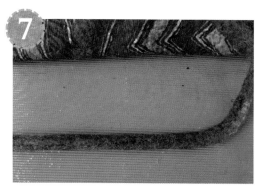

Continue working along the length of the handle, pulling as well as rolling. This helps to stretch the handle to increase the length.

Once the handle is evenly firm along its length, you are ready to carry on felting the rest of the bag.

Continue to felt by rolling, throwing and scrunching as explained previously, warming the work as necessary until the bag is fully felted and shrunk to the desired size, in this example, 39cm × 27cm (15.6in × 10.8in). Rinse and shape your bag. This example has a stitched magnetic clasp but you might consider using a button instead.

THE FINISHING TOUCHES

Once you have fully felted your bag, rinse out all the soap and spin dry it if you have a spin dryer. If you do not have a spin dryer, squeeze out as much water as possible by hand. Roll your felt in a thick, clean towel, put it on the floor and trample it until the towel has absorbed as much water as possible. It is important not to leave the bag to dry flat as it will retain that form. Shape the bag, forcefully stretching it out with your hands or wooden formers to make it three-dimensional. Stuff it with bubble wrap, newspapers or a towel, pushing into any corners. Rub over with a plastic bag to smooth the fibres. As the bag dries, you can tweak and pull it into shape. Leave to dry thoroughly before removing any excess fluff on the surface (you can shave it away) and visible threads. A gentle pressing with an iron also helps to smooth the surface and remove excess hairs.

PROJECT ▶ SMALL BAG WITH INTEGRAL FLAT HANDLE

The edges of the flap and handle have been machine-stitched on this bag to add definition and the extra flap section was cut and hand-stitched to form an inside pocket.

This is another basic bag that is quick to make, where you can play around with the shape. In order to obtain a reasonable length of handle you will end up with a large flap so there may be no need for a clasp. You can experiment with the decoration, perhaps adding some stitched elements as it will be a feature of the bag. Keep the handle section of the resist curved. If you add an extra layer of wool around the handle area, it will make it stronger, which you can then stretch to lengthen it. However, for a larger bag, where you require a more durable handle, look at the projects in Chapter 7.

The measurements of the resist are as follows: AB = 45cm (18in), CD = 35cm (14in), EF = 40cm (16in), GH = 30cm (12in). This was covered with two layers of Corriedale wool in turquoise then two layers in black. With this

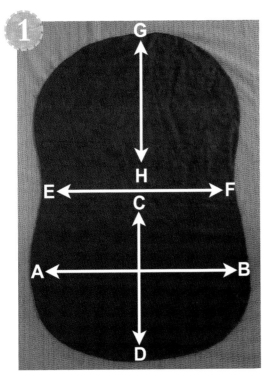

The top half of the resist needs to be almost the same as the bottom half otherwise your handle will be small.

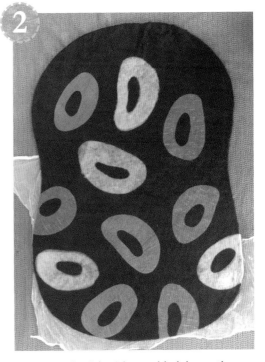

Leave 3cm (1.2in) with no added decoration around the top edge of the bag as this will form the handle.

Leave the top half of the front of the bag undecorated as this section will be cut away.

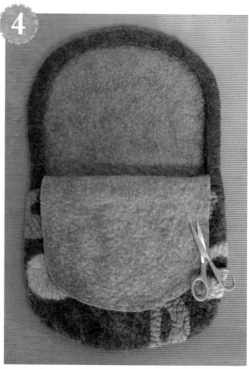

Remember to shape your bag and lay it flat before cutting.

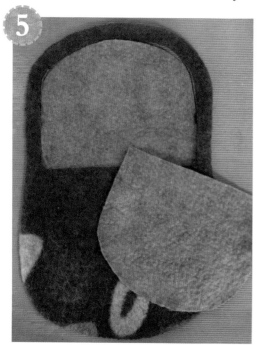

Take care to match up the front and the back and cut the correct section. Do NOT cut off the flap.

method of working, you can really experiment with colour and pattern. I used simple pebble shapes in an open weave linen and needlefelt. Felt the bag as described previously until it is almost fully felted. Mark a line 2.5–3cm (1–1.2in) from the edge of the top half of the bag and cut through on one side. Turn the bag over and repeat on the other side but this time cut straight across. With soapy hands, open out the handle section so it lies flat, gently pull, rub and stretch until it is straight and firm.

Continue to felt by rolling, throwing and scrunching as explained previously, warming the work as necessary until the bag is fully felted and shrunk to the desired size. Rinse and shape the bag.

PROJECT ▶ CIRCULAR BAG WITH SEPARATE CORD HANDLE AND CONCEALED MAGNETIC CLASP

very dark brown so, when felted, the colour is a blend of the two.

Make a cord handle as described in Chapter 5.

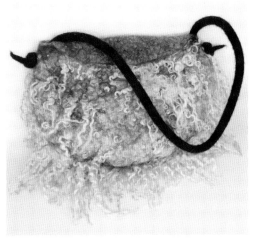

The raw wool decoration dramatically transforms the look of a very basic design.

Working with uncarded fleece

Ensure that the wool fibres are fully wetted down and are tight to the edge of the resist before starting your decoration.

You can create a huge variety of bags with a simple circle resist by altering the way you add the flap, handle and decoration. It is an ideal starting point for your first large bag and provides an ample surface to decorate. For this example, I chose to use unwashed and uncarded fleece to demonstrate the technique. However, I would not recommend using this until you are confident with your feltmaking skills. I started with a 50cm (20in) diameter resist with four layers of wool; two of Roux d'Ardenne (a French breed) and two of Welsh Black. I chose these wools in batt form as they are strong wools and are compatible with adding the uncarded fleece decoration. For a beginner, I would recommend using merino, Corriedale or Shetland and use the same wool for all four layers although you can use different colours. I enjoy experimenting with mixing wools to create extra texture due to the different shrinkage rates and to blend the colours for a richness and depth. The Roux d'Ardenne is a pale ruddy beige and the Welsh Black is a

Using raw (uncarded) fleece is a wonderful way of adding an extra dimension to your work. However, it does entail some degree of skill and patience so I will explain a simple method of using it. There are many methods of using raw fleece, which are worth exploring as you progress through your feltmaking journey. I have used Wensleydale locks here as the staple is fabulously long, soft and curly and easily felts in with other wools. Preparing the wool fibres takes some time so I would do this in advance. You need to remove any excess dirt and material first, then distinguish the shorn edge from the end curls. At the shorn edge, you need to slowly ease and open out the fibres so they will felt to the surface of your bag. Do make sure that you wash your hands after handling raw wool, especially when touching your face or eating and drinking.

Lay the locks, with the shorn edge innermost and the locks extending over the edge of

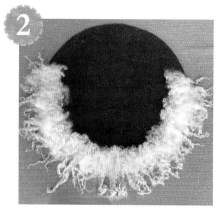

You may just want to have a fringe on the edge of your bag and add different decoration in the centre. You can add wisps of the base fibre over the shorn ends to help anchor them.

Take care in laying your locks down evenly when filling in to prevent clumps that will not felt in.

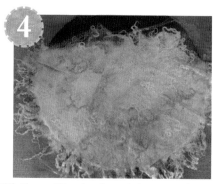

With the netting in place, take some time with the rubbing to ensure that the raw locks stay in place. Do not rub the loose locks at the edge as you want them to retain their curls.

the bag. Then fill in the centre ensuring that you are not creating any big 'clumps' of wool. Leave a 3–5cm (1.2–2in) gap at the top edge for the flap. Lay netting over the surface and gently rub with soapy hands until the shorn edge fibres are fixed in place and not lifting – you do not necessarily want the curls to felt in but the ends do need to be anchored down. Turn over and repeat on the other side. Before you start rolling, to help the shorn ends migrate through the base wool fibres, hold the edges of the mat or bubble wrap and gently flip the bag by lifting it approximately 5–10cm (2–4in) off the table and dropping it back down, rotating it and working on all sides. Make sure that you are not moving the fibres away from the resist. Turn over and repeat. Gently lift the ends of the locks to check that they are anchored to the bag. Continue massaging if they are still loose. Once they are securely anchored, you can start rolling.

Continue to felt the bag, rolling first with the noodle. Check occasionally that the shorn ends are felting in but also lift the curly ends so they do not felt in. Once the wool fibres are starting to shrink, you can warm the bag and start to scrunch and throw. With this technique of decoration, it is best to throw at this

stage for the fibres to mix and migrate. Constantly check and lift the curls: you may need to trim any clumpy bits or remove loose fibres. Continue to felt until the bag is almost fully felted.

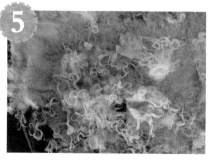

Constantly check that shorn ends are felting in but also that the curls are not.

Finishing the bag

Cut open the top of the bag; just under a third of the diameter makes a reasonably sized opening. Trim to make a neat edge. Continue to felt the bag until it is properly fulled and the edges are sealed. To fit the cord handle, make two holes 3cm (1.2in) to either side of the flap using an awl or knitting needle. Enlarge the hole by rotating the awl or needle. Avoid cutting it; if it is too large you cannot make it smaller but you can make it larger. Rinse the bag really well before adding the cord handle, fold over the top to form a cuff, shape and leave to dry.

The finished bag was fitted with a magnetic clasp with tabs. The folded-over cuff at the top of the bag conceals the tabs.

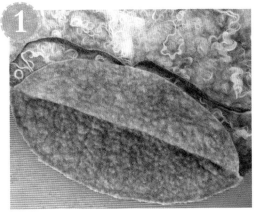

To keep the edges even, mark with a watercolour pencil before you cut.

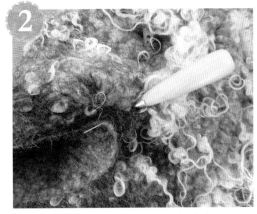

Gently rotate the awl to widen the hole.

Ease the cord handle through the hole when it is wet; a tight fit is desirable so the handle will not slip out.

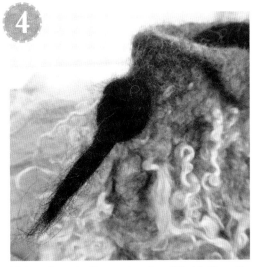

Make a knot in the cord and pull tight. Once it is dry, secure the knot with a few stitches of strong thread to hold it in place, especially if the bag will be used to hold heavy items.

ADVANCED DESIGNS

The projects in this chapter introduce more complex techniques using book resists and additional, separate resists. Working in this way takes extra time and planning but the results are worth the effort. Once you understand the function of a book resist, the possibilities are limitless and can be developed further to make more elaborate sculptural forms. As the designs become more complex, it is even more important to remember to make notes and take photographs of your progress.

PROJECT ▶ ADAPTABLE BAG WITH INTEGRAL FLAT HANDLE AND SLOT FASTENING

Using Bergschaf wool creates a strong bag that will endure daily use.

This design is very flexible. Although it takes time and concentration to lay down the fibres, the felting process is quick and it requires little finishing at the end. You can play around with the flap shape, adapt the fastening method, or add a pocket.

Making the resist

The resist consists of three components: the handle, the flap and the main bag. You can experiment with the shape of each component to create a variety of bag shapes. In this example, AB = 50cm (20in), CD = 32cm (12.8in), EF = 15cm (7.5in) and GH = 5.5cm (2.2in). Rather than starting from scratch, make a paper template using these dimensions, then adjust them to create your own design. To save time, fold a piece of paper in half and draw one half of the bag, then when you cut it out, the shape will be symmetrical. Once you are happy with the shape you can transfer it to your resist material. Using masking tape on both sides of the resist, stick the handle and the flap to the main bag resist, separately (not with one length of masking tape) as the flap resist is removed before the handle resist.

Left: A longer handle will make your bag more versatile.

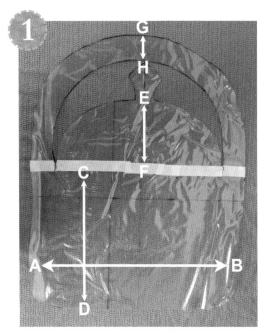

Make sure that there is a gap between the handle and flap resists for ease of laying out.

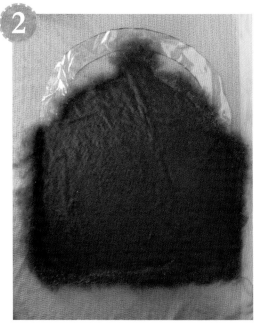

Lay two layers of wool over the flap and bag resists with a fringe extending 2.5cm (1in) over the edges. Wet down, keeping the fringe edges dry.

Laying down the wool

Lay down the wool methodically and in sequence so you do not lose track of your progress. It is worth taking a note of which layer and which side you are on as you go along. There are six layers on each side of the flap and main bag resists and four on each side of the handle resist. For this example, I used Bergschaf wool in two colours with a merino decoration. The final two layers (layers five and six on the main bag and three and four on the handle) are in a different colour. Place the cord fastening before the final two layers on the bag.

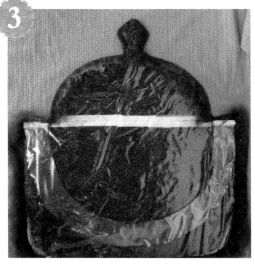

Turn over, pull the handle resist down and fold the fringe over the flap, easing out any creases. Return the handle resist and fold over the fringe on the bottom of the bag resist. Place a piece of thin plastic folded in half along the join of the flap and the bag resist.

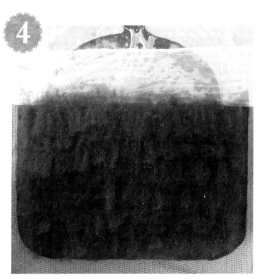

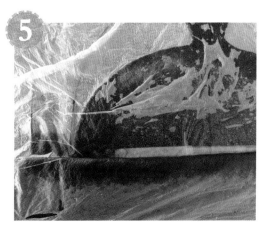

Meeting the folded fringe at the bottom of the bag, lay down two layers of wool with a very fine fringe extending just above the line where the bag and flap resists join. Wet down and lay down another two layers of wool with a fringe extending over the edges of the bottom of the bag.

After wetting the wool down, pull the thin plastic down to form a neat fold. Remove the plastic and gently ease the folded fibres over the handle resist back along the handle (the folded edge should only be on the opening of the bag).

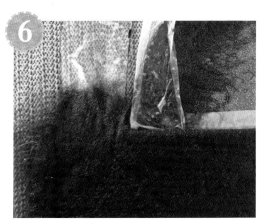

Insert a small piece of thin plastic under the fold at each edge to prevent the flap from felting to the bag opening. Carefully turn the bag over, making sure that you grip the whole bag as you do not want the resists to separate.

After folding in the fringe, lay down a further two layers of wool with a very fine fringe at the flap edge. Wet down, turn over and fold over the fringe on the flap.

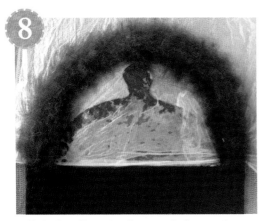

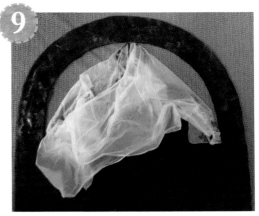

Pull the handle resist down and place a piece of thin plastic over the flap, then return the handle resist. Lay down two layers of wool over the handle with a small fringe extending over the edges. Wet down and turn over.

Pull the plastic away so you can fold over the fringe and lay down two layers of wool to meet the fringe. Repeat Steps 6 and 7 in the final colour, so you have four layers of wool on the handle resist.

Making the cord for the fastening

Mark the position of the fastening with a watercolour pencil; this needs to be a little lower than the depth of the flap, which in this example is 16cm (6.4in) down from the top of the bag opening in the centre of the bag. Lay down two layers of wool and remark the fastening position.

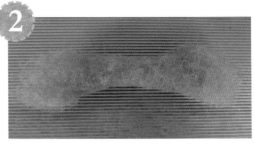

Measure the thinnest part of your flap toggle, 7cm (2.8in) in this example. Add 2.5cm (1in) at each end and lay down a row of wool fibres on a rubber mat or bubble wrap. Roll up in the centre as if you are making a cord handle.

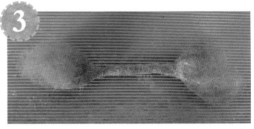

Wet just the centre and roll as explained in Chapter 5 for the cord handle until it is felted firmly.

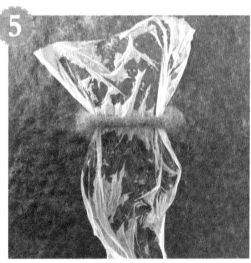

Open out the dry fibres at each end of the fastening and place in position.

Place a piece of thin plastic underneath the fastening to prevent it from felting to the bag.

Gently fold the fringe of the final layer inside the bag to form a neat edge.

Decoration

At this stage you can add your choice of decoration. Focusing on the flap and the back of the bag so the pattern appears more prominent, I used four colours of merino, which I cut and laid down in stripes adding some pencil roving on top.

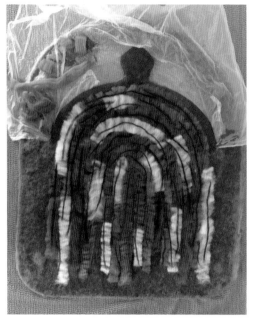

Do bear in mind the shape of your bag. The flap is the most prominent element, so I have just focused on decorating this area.

Once you have applied the decoration, you are ready to start felting the bag. Massage well with bubble wrap on top then with soapy hands directly on the wool to settle the fibres. Ensure they are tight against the resist before you start rolling. Roll gently at the beginning – you do not want to dislodge the different resist components. Keep checking your progress. Once you see some slight shrinkage against the resist (usually after about 200 rolls with the noodle), it is time to remove the flap resist. Carefully unpeel the masking tape and ease out the flap resist. Smooth down the fringe on the flap with soapy hands. Continue to roll until you can see the resist pulling at the edges. Remove the tape attaching the handle resist to the bag and very carefully remove the handle resist.

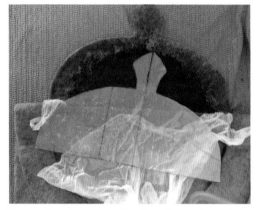

Be gentle when removing the flap resist as it is very easy to pull the bag out of shape at this stage.

Felting the handle

Take extra care when removing the handle resist as you do not want to distort the handle's shape.

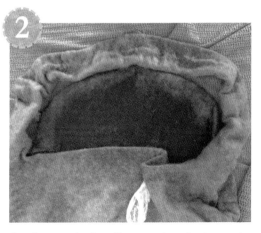

Gently ease the handle around so the top and bottom edges meet in the centre and it lies flat (the ridges are now the centre of the handle). Slowly work your way along the handle and rub with soapy hands to join the two sides together.

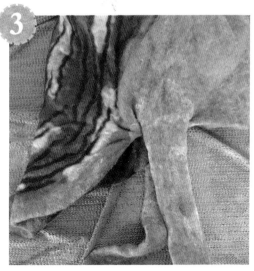

Work on the middle section of the handle first before moving to the ends attached to the bag. You will need to take extra time here, easing out the sides with soapy hands so the handle lies flat.

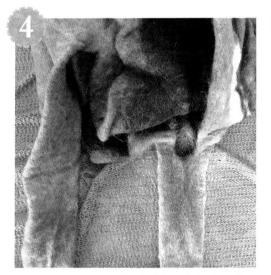

Continue to massage both sides of the handle, slowly increasing the pressure, until it feels firm and the centre fibres are no longer moving.

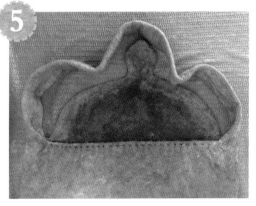

You may need to stitch the top of the bag as described in Chapter 4 to pull it in, so it does not gape when the flap is pulled over to the front.

Continue to felt the bag, warming when necessary, then start to full by rolling, throwing and scrunching. Carefully stretch the handle to lengthen it. Finish the bag as described in Chapter 6.

PROJECT ▶ SHOPPING BAG WITH ATTACHED CORD HANDLES AND EXTERIOR POCKET, USING A BOOK RESIST, MASKING TAPE AND SURFACE RESISTS

This is a complex project and will take the best part of two days to complete, using a combination of coarser wools, Swaledale and Shetland for strength and durability.

Making the resist

Prepare your design in advance, working out the size and proportions, and sketch your finished bag. The shape of this bag is a rectangle with sloping sides, smaller at the base and wider at the open top. The bottom has 45-degree corner triangles, which create a flat rectangle at the bottom of the bag. You need to work out the height of your bag, the width at the bottom and top, and the width of the base and gusset. The resist size in this example is AB = 57cm (22.8in), CD = 50cm (20in), EF = 50cm (20in) and the base and gusset width is 8.5cm (3.4in).

BOOK RESISTS

Rather than using a single resist, a book resist adds extra 'leaves' or 'pages', hence the name, to create three-dimensional form. They are wonderful for creating intricate sculptural shapes and can be utilized for forming a gusset in a bag. Using a book resist gives you the advantage of creating a definite form with minimal shaping by hand. Master using a single resist before embarking on a project using a book resist. Allow adequate quiet and uninterrupted time as you need to concentrate and not rush. As it is easy to confuse the position of your 'leaves', get into the habit of folding over the fringes when you turn the work over (ensuring that you are only folding over a single leaf and not two stuck together) before laying down any further layers of wool. This makes it much easier to keep track. Round off any sharp corners on your resist as they have a tendency to poke through the wool and create weak points in your bag.

Many techniques have been incorporated in this bag; the larger size makes an ideal canvas for experimenting with decoration.

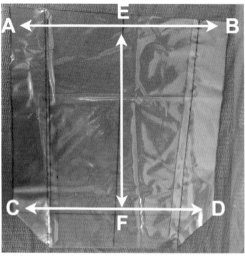

Add an extra 2.5cm (1in) to the inside edge of the gusset pieces and stitch to the main bag section with a running stitch using a strong thread.

Laying down the wool

Lay two layers of wool over the entire surface on one side – in this example I used Swaledale. Wet down, keeping the edges dry. Cover with thin plastic, pressing down firmly so it 'sticks' to the wool, and gently ease open a gusset leaf. Fold over the fringe, rubbing with the edge of your soap to make sure the fibres are tight to the resist. Ease out any folds at the points. Cover the gusset with thin plastic and fold back. Repeat on the other gusset and turn the bag over.

Fold over the fringe at the top and bottom of the bag and lay down two layers of wool meeting these edges but extending over the edges of the gussets. Wet down and fold over the fringes on the gussets as on the first side. Lay down two layers of wool on each of the gusset leaves meeting the folded-over fringe,

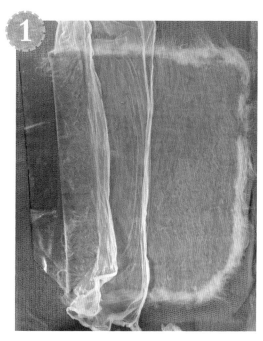

Ensure that you tuck your fringe over the gusset before working on the other side.

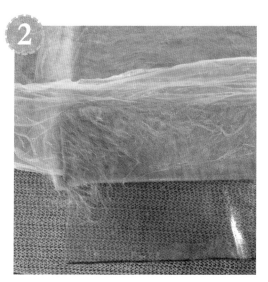

Where the leaf is stitched at the top and bottom of the bag, carefully divide the fibres between the front and back.

Covering the bag with thin plastic keeps the fibres in place as you open and close the leaves.

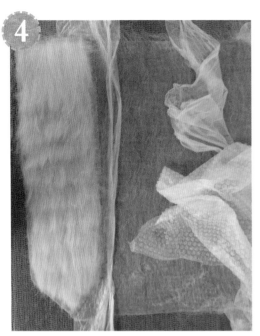

When using a resist for the first time, it can be a little stiff, so make sure that the leaves lie flat when you open them out.

wetting down and covering with thin plastic. Lay down a further two layers of wool in exactly the same way as the first two layers. There should now be four layers on both sides and gussets.

Making the cord handles

Refer to the instructions in Chapter 5 and make two cord handles keeping both ends dry so you can attach them to the bag. This example is 80cm long for a finished 50cm length using Swaledale and Shetland wool.

Lay three rows of the wool (for the outside of the handle) vertically. Lay the top layer horizontally leaving a frame around the edge.

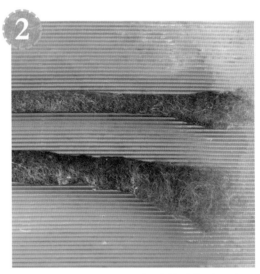

The cords do not need to be fully felted as they will continue to felt in the next stages of making the bag. Making two identical handles will be good practice for you.

Handles, decoration and pocket

This design has an outside pocket and resist decoration. It is important to prepare all these elements plus your handles before laying down the final layers of wool on the bag. Attach the handles first as their position will dictate where you decorate the bag. Mark the centre of the bag with a watercolour pencil and measure out from there to ensure equal placement. Spread out the dry ends of one handle and place on the bag, leaving at least 5cm from the top edge to allow for trimming. The pocket is created with a circle resist 23cm (9.2in) in diameter, covered on one side with two layers of wool (the inside of the pocket) and the other side with four layers of wool, using different colours for each side as a decorative feature and a way of identifying each side. Place this towards the top of the bag with the four-layer side uppermost. For the resist decoration, I covered two circles, 18cm (7.29in) and 11cm (4.4in) in diameter with two layers of wool on each side, each circle in a different colour. Place the smaller circle down first with the larger one over the top.

Using masking tape as a resist

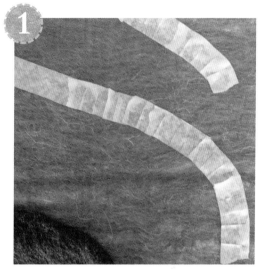

Mark out the position of the tape with watercolour pencil, leaving plenty of space at the top and bottom of the bag. Use 2.5cm (1in) tape, snipping it into short lengths and overlapping them to create curves. Take care when placing the masking tape as the fibres will lift if you need to move it.

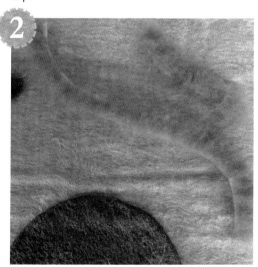

Lay two layers of wool over the masking tape and wet down. It is easier to use batts to cover small areas as the staple is shorter.

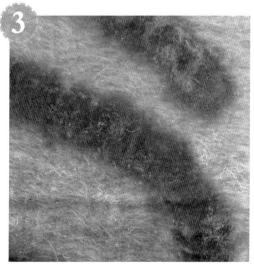

Once wetted down, you can ease the fibres into place over the masking tape and fill in any gaps.

Laying down the final two layers of wool

Check that all your decorative elements and handle are in place before laying down the final two layers of wool.

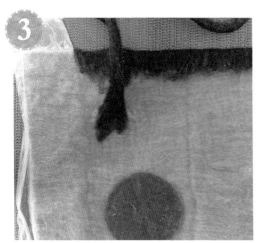

Carefully fill in the area underneath the handle without pulling it out of place.

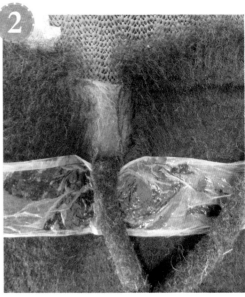

Fold over the fringe before placing the handles on the other side of the bag. Note the smaller circle decoration in place here.

Take care when turning your work over at this stage. Grip it firmly as it will be wet and heavy. The larger circle decoration has now been placed over the smaller one.

Lay down two layers of wool in exactly the same way as the first two layers but avoid laying any wool over the upper section of the cord handles. Wet down and place a piece of thin plastic over the area where the handles join the bag so they can be folded down to lay fibres underneath. Lay another piece of thin plastic down before moving the handle back to prevent it felting to the top of the bag. Turn the bag over and add the handles and decoration on the other side.

Once you have laid down all six layers of wool, massage all four sides, firstly with bubble wrap over the top, and then with soapy hands so that the wool fibres are tight to the edges of the resist and they are stable. It is very important to do this when using book resists otherwise ridges may form. Now felt the bag as described previously, taking care when moving it that you do not dislodge the handles. Once the resist starts to pull at the edges, you can push it to the centre of the bag and gently ease out the gussets. Keep moving it around as you roll. Keep felting until the bag is almost fully felted. Reshape the bag, laying it flat. Mark first with a water-colour pencil and cut open the top.

When rolling, make sure that you regularly move the flaps to prevent ridges from forming.

To keep a straight edge, cut across the two sides together.

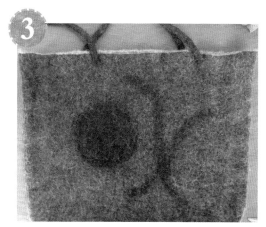

By using different colours of wool for your resist decoration, their position is quite obvious.

Cutting the circle resist

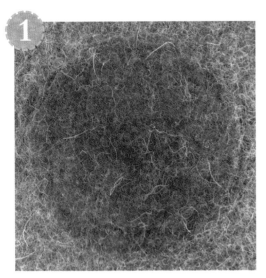

Mark the centre of the circle with a watercolour pencil then draw a small circle. It is best not to cut too large a hole as you can make it larger by stretching.

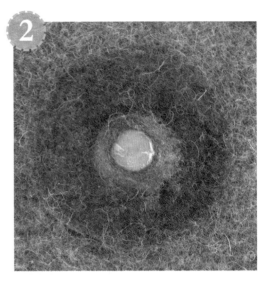

Cut out the circle, soap the edges and rub, easing out as you go. Remove the resist and massage the circle with soapy hands to form into a spherical shape.

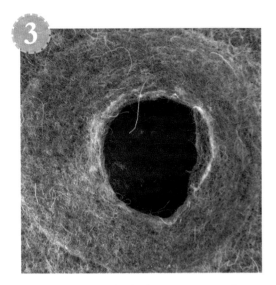

Mark the inner resist in the same way and repeat as with the top resist but cutting a smaller circle this time. Work on both circles until you are happy with the shape.

Cutting the masking tape resist

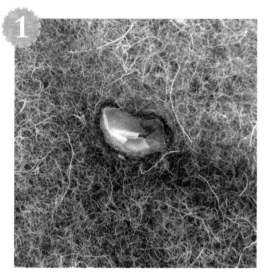

Cut a small line in the centre of the resist line and check that you can see the masking tape before cutting any further.

Push a pen along the masking tape to indicate where to cut along the centre line.

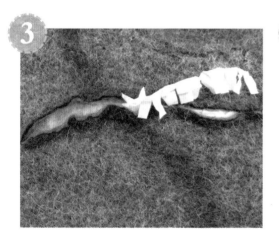

Remove the tape and rub down any raised fibres with a soapy finger.

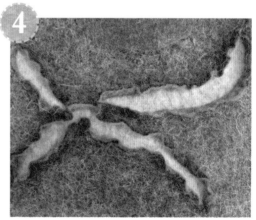

Pull the edges of the cut edge to reveal the colour underneath and form a frilly edge if desired.

Cutting the pocket edge

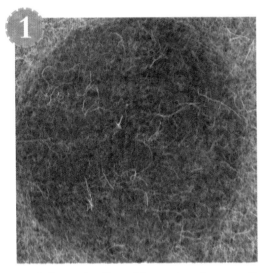

Mark the cutting line with a watercolour pencil before you cut, slightly in from the edge of the circle and just down from the top.

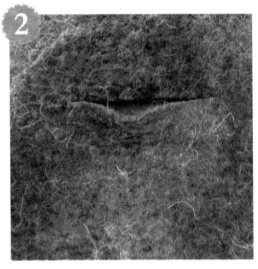

Cut along the line and carefully remove the resist.

Warm up the bag and continue to full, rolling, throwing and scrunching. Rub the handles with soapy hands and work on the circle resist area. Continue until the edges are felted and sealed. Rinse and finish as described before.

Shape the circle and masking tape decoration pattern while the bag is still wet.

PROJECT ▶ SHOULDER BAG USING A BOOK RESIST WITH AN ATTACHED FLAT HANDLE, CORD TOGGLE FASTENING AND MASKING TAPE RESIST

Although this project takes time, the end result produces a hard-wearing and functional bag.

It takes time to prepare all the elements and to lay out but, as with the first bag in this chapter, the actual felting of this bag does not take long. Attaching the handle separately allows you to adjust the length. In this example, I have made a long handle so the bag can be worn over the shoulder. You will need to make the handle, pocket and cord toggle fastening first. I used Bergschaf wool for this project. It is one of my favourite wools, quick to felt and hard-wearing. I selected three shades of green, so the colours would blend to give a richness to the finished bag (and changing colour between every two layers makes it easier to keep track of the number of layers in the process) with a masking tape resist texture.

Preparing the handle

You will need a long surface to work on to make this handle. Using the method explained in Chapter 5, I laid down a 125cm (50in) length and 24cm (9.6in) width of wool fibre aiming for a finished length of 100cm (40in) and a width of 4cm (1.6in). Remembering to leave both ends dry, felt until it is a firm pre-felt.

Preparing the pocket

Decide on your pocket shape and size and lay down four layers of wool fibre on one side of the resist, tucking the fringe over the edge. In this example I have used a round pocket 22cm (8.8in) in diameter covering all edges of the resist. For a square or rectangular pocket, follow the instructions for the Clutch Bag in Chapter 4.

Preparing the fastening

If you choose to use a cord toggle fastening for this bag, you will need to prepare it in advance. In this example, I made a small cord with dry ends and a longer cord (about 20cm (8in)) with one dry end.

Making the resist

The shape of this bag is a tapering rectangular box, wider at the bottom than at the top. A rectangular shape would work too, with straight rather than sloping sides. The top and bottom have 45-degree corner triangles, which creates a rectangular box at the top and bottom of the bag. This example is made from two pieces of plastic resist stitched together along the gusset edge. However, to save plastic, you can make the gussets separately as described in the Shopping Bag project (page 86). AB = 24cm (9.6in), CD = 55cm (22in), with a shaped gusset, 8cm (3.2in) at the bottom reducing to 4cm (1.6in) at the top.

Starting the bag

Place your pocket with the fringe side uppermost before laying down your first two layers of wool. Lay down four layers in total in the same way as explained in the Shopping Bag instructions.

Carefully plan where the handles will be placed as this will affect where the flap will be cut and the positioning of the fastening. AB is equal to half CD. This will affect the position of your decoration too.

Make sure that you place the pocket above the bottom section of the resist and below where the flap will be cut.

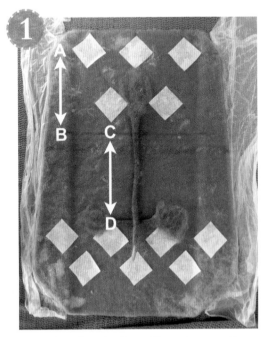

Remember that the flap will overlap a section of your bag and obscure any decoration.

If using a masking tape resist, lay it down before attaching the fastening. I have used rectangles of masking tape, which will be cut open to form circular craters.

Attaching the fastening

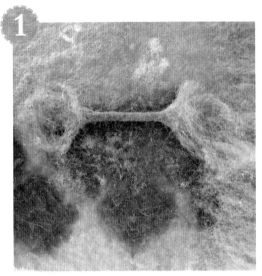

Do not forget to place two layers of wool underneath your cord fastening and fan out the dry ends of wool fibre.

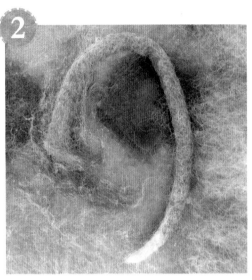

Try to spread out the dry wool fibres at the base of the cord evenly either side so it will be well secured.

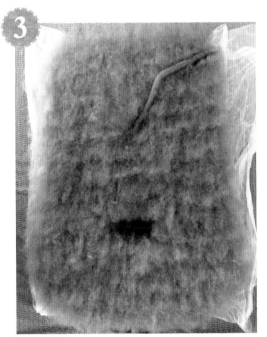

Lay down the final two layers of wool fibre carefully around the cord fastening.

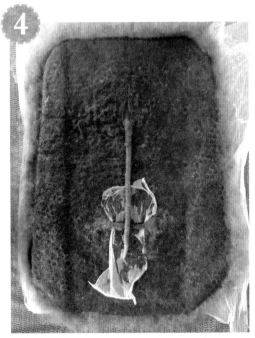

Wet down and insert a piece of thin plastic underneath the cord fastenings.

Usually I advise folding over the edges on the gusset before working on the reverse of the bag. In this case, as the handles are attached to the gussets, it is easier to complete the decoration on the back and front before adding them.

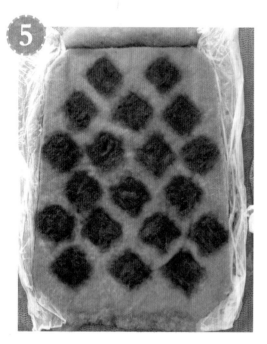

Place the masking tape resist and top colour before folding over the top and bottom fringes to ensure that the correct colours are revealed when cut open.

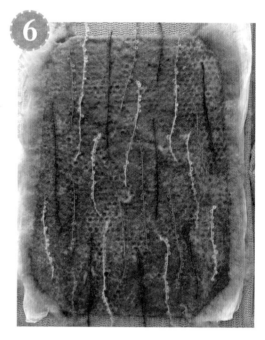

After laying down the final two layers, further decoration can be added. Make sure it wraps around the top edge and bottom edges.

Placing the handles

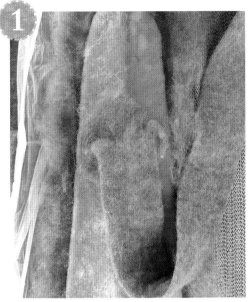

Open out the gusset and mark where the handle is to be placed to align just below where the flap will be cut. Divide the dry wool at the ends of the bag into two, open out and place on the gusset.

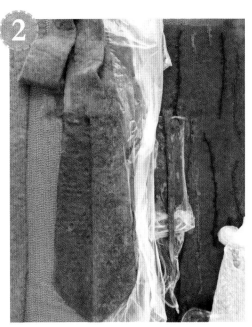

Fold over the fringe and carefully fill in with two layers of wool.

Repeat at the other end of the gusset, taking care not to lift the handle.

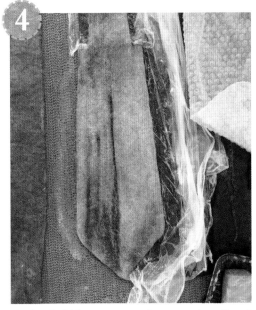

Placing bubble wrap over the top, rub well and then massage with soapy hands until the fibres are settled and not moving.

It is vital that you take time to secure the first end of the handle before moving on to the second end. The bag will be wet and heavy so the handles are at risk of being dislodged. Repeat on the other side checking that the handle is not twisted.

Once the handle is secure at both ends, work on the back and front of the bag by massaging with bubble wrap on top and then with soapy hands so that the wool fibres are stable and not moving before you start rolling. Roll with a noodle, gently to start with, rotating and moving the gusset flaps regularly to ensure that ridges do not form. Once the bag begins to shrink, push the resist away from the edge and continue to roll. Carry on the felting process until the bag has almost fully felted. Pull the bag into shape before cutting the flap. Mark the cutting line from the base of each side of the handle and underneath the cord fastening. Cut this line first before cutting the gusset flaps. Cut the gusset tabs and open out the flap. Trim the flap to the desired shape and round off the gusset tabs. Remove the resists and massage the pocket to make sure that it is evenly felted; it sometimes needs a little extra work as the outside of the bag has had more friction applied than the inside. A circular pocket will need an opening cut as described in the Shopping Bag instructions.

Take care that you shape the bag into a rectangular form before cutting the flap.

Mark the gusset flaps slightly smaller than the flap.

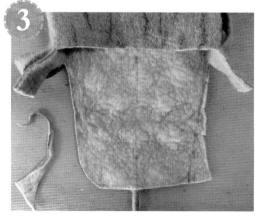

Mark and check lines before cutting; mistakes can be hard to rectify.

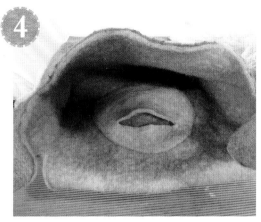

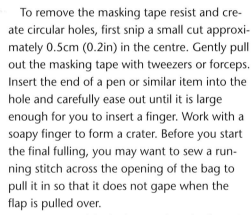

I made the pocket in a brighter colour so it is easy to locate inside the bag.

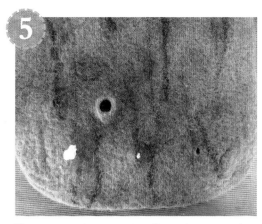

If you use a strong contrasting colour over the masking tape resist in comparison to the final layers of wool, then it will be clearly evident where the resists are placed.

To remove the masking tape resist and create circular holes, first snip a small cut approximately 0.5cm (0.2in) in the centre. Gently pull out the masking tape with tweezers or forceps. Insert the end of a pen or similar item into the hole and carefully ease out until it is large enough for you to insert a finger. Work with a soapy finger to form a crater. Before you start the final fulling, you may want to sew a running stitch across the opening of the bag to pull it in so that it does not gape when the flap is pulled over.

Continue to felt the bag as described previously until the edges are felted. Rub the handles with soapy hands and stretch to lengthen if necessary. Check and open out the circle craters regularly. Rinse and finish, pulling out all the circle craters and leave to dry.

CONCLUSION

Congratulations on reaching the end of this book. I hope it has inspired you to continue to make felt and embark on new projects to learn different techniques. Feltmaking is addictive – the longer I make felt, the more I discover there is to learn. Experiment and develop your own way of working to create your own fabulous designs, which will be unique to you.

Feltmaking is a physical process and therefore difficult to describe in words; I have tried to keep the instructions simple and clear. However, there is no substitute for a hands-on workshop where a tutor can demonstrate the correct feel and texture of each stage of the feltmaking process. They can help you when you go wrong or are unsure if you are doing the right thing. So, use this book in conjunction with attending physical workshops to fully develop your feltmaking skills – feltmakers are a friendly bunch; you will make new friends and learn new tricks. Maybe our paths will cross. The important thing is to have fun!

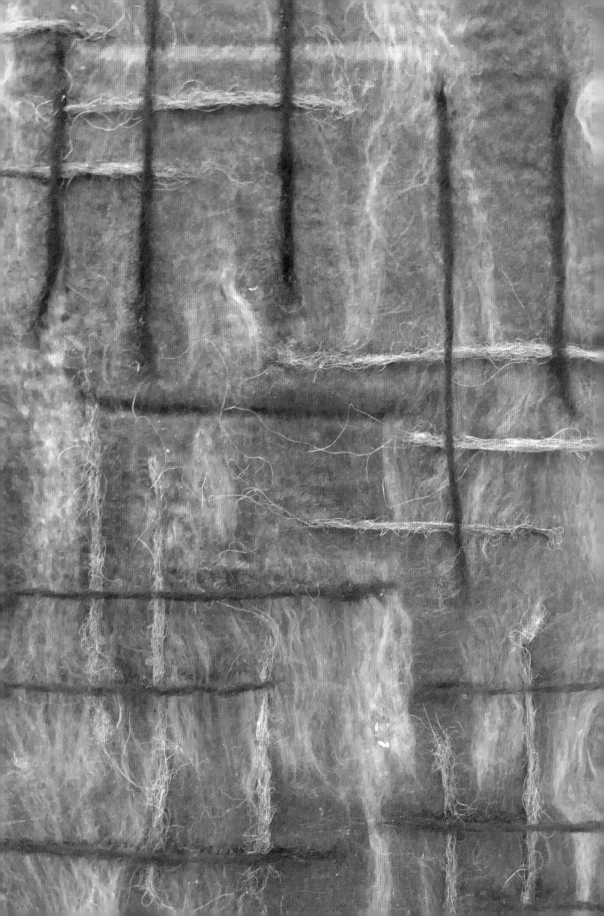

GLOSSARY

Batts: fleece that has been lifted directly from the carding machine as loose fibres.

Carders: these can be small hand-held tools or large machines, which have small hooks that comb the wool fibres into the same direction.

Crimp: the natural waviness of the fibres.

Felt: a non-woven fabric created by applying moisture, heat and friction to wool fibres.

Fibre: the individual strands of wool.

Fleece: the shorn wool of the sheep.

Fulling: the final felting process where the wool is shrunk to a firm and tight fabric.

Laminated felt: also known as applied or nuno felt, where wool fibre and woven fabrics are combined together.

Laying down: creating rows of shingles to make layers of wool before wetting down.

Micron: the measurement used for the thickness of the fibre, equal to one millionth of a metre.

Needlefelt: sometimes called punched felt, this is a mechanical, waterless process where fleece is punched repetitively with barbed needles to form a flat sheet.

Nepps: these are small nodules of wool or cotton that are the waste material from spinning yarn; they are used for decoration.

Pre-felt: sometimes known as half-felt, it refers to the first stage of the feltmaking process where the fibres have tangled enough to stay together but before any real shrinking has taken place.

Resist: a material such as fabric or plastic that prevents the wool from felting to itself.

Rolling: a method of applying friction to the wool, encouraging the fibres to mesh together.

Roving: the same as wool tops.

Scales: these cover the surface of the wool fibres, smooth in one direction, rough in the opposite. The size and hardness of the scales affects the ability of the wool to felt and the quality of the felt.

Scouring: the cleaning process for shorn fleece to remove dirt, vegetation and grease before carding.

Scrunching: squeezing and rubbing the wool with soapy hands once it has reached the pre-felt stage to encourage shrinkage.

Shingle: a fine tuft of wool pulled from roving.

Throwing: a method of applying friction to the wool, encouraging the fibres to mesh together.

Tops: a rope of wool that has been combed so that all the fibres lie in one direction and the shorter fibres have been removed.

Tufts: see shingle.

Two layers: two layers of fibres laid down at right angles to each other.

Wetting down: applying warm, soapy water ensuring that the fibres are fully wet.

Left: Detail of the pattern of the clutch bag in Chapter 4; once felted the effect is far subtler.

FURTHER READING

Many good books on feltmaking are now out of print. Some, such as Mary Burkett's classic listed below, are worth seeking out. However, methods of making have changed over the years so older books do not always cover all the newer developments. There are many inspirational books available too that may not offer practical advice but are good investments.

BOOKS

Ascher, Shirley and Jane Bateman (2006). *Beginner's Guide to Feltmaking*. Search Press.
Burkett, M.E. (1979). *The Art of the Felt Maker*. Abbot Hall Art Gallery.
Houghton, Lizzie (2009). *Felting Fashion: Creative and Inspirational Techniques for Feltmakers*. Batsford.
Johnson, Jorie (2006). *Feltmaking and Wool Magic: Contemporary Techniques and Beautiful Projects*. Rockport Publishers.
Mackay, Moy (2012). *Art in Felt and Stitch*. Search Press.
McGavock, Deborah and Christine Lewis (2000). *Feltmaking*. The Crowood Press.
Smith, Sheila (2006). *Felt to Stitch: Creative Felting for Textile Artists*. Batsford.
White, Christine (2007). *Uniquely Felt*. Storey.

USEFUL WEBSITES

International Feltmakers Association

This is a not-for-profit, non-selective organization established to promote felt in all its forms, welcoming everyone with an interest in feltmaking from the beginner to the professional. The website is a valuable resource where feltmakers worldwide can find useful information, advice, insights, resources and inspiration for developing their feltmaking skills and broadening their networks. There is a members' gallery and up-to-date listings of felt workshops, exhibitions and events.
www.feltmakers.com

British Wool

Formerly the British Wool Marketing Board, this website provides an extensive insight into British wool breeds and their use.
www.britishwool.org.uk

Left: This shoulder bag, a project from Chapter 7, has the same decoration back and front.

LIST OF SUPPLIERS

SUPPLIERS OF FIBRES AND FELTMAKING EQUIPMENT

UK

Adelaide Walker
Unit 22, Town Head Mills, Addingham, Ilkley
LS29 0PD.
+44 (0)1943 830600
enquiries@adelaidewalker.co.uk
www.adelaidewalker.co.uk

Norwegian Wool at Artisan Felt and Stitch
2 New Street, Carnforth, LA5 9BX
+44 (0)7703 682389
info@norwegianwool.co.uk
www.norwegianwool.co.uk

Wingham Wool Work
70 Main Street, Wentworth, Rotherham, South
Yorkshire S62 7TN
+44 (0)1226 742926
mail@winghamwoolwork.co.uk
www.winghamwoolwork.co.uk

World of Wool
Unit 8, The Old Railway Goods Yard, Scar
Lane, Milnsbridge, Huddersfield HD3 4PE
+44 (0)3300 564888
info@worldofwool.co.uk
www.worldofwool.co.uk

Left: A variation of the oval bag from Chapter 6,
using Black Welsh wool with alpaca and flax
surface decoration.

Europe

DHG Shop
+39 (0)574 1662721
info@dhgshop.it
www.dhgshop.it

Wollknoll GmbH
Forsthausstrasse 7, 74420 Oberrot-Neuhausen,
Germany
+49 (0)7977 910293
info@wollknoll.de
www.wollknoll.eu

Meaningful Crafts
Wezenland 1, 1791 AZ Den Burg (Texel), The
Netherlands
+31 (0)222 313644
hi@meaningfulcrafts.com
www.meaningfulcrafts.com

Piiku
Piesalantilantie 17, 41900 Petäjävesi, Finland
+353 (0)40 847 4424
info@piiku.fi
www.piiku.fi

Australia

Fibre Fusion
PO Box 67, Kew East, Victoria 3102, Australia
+(0)61 3 9859 8081
www.fibrefusion.com.au

USA

Outback Fibers
PO Box 55, Coaldale, CO 81222, USA
www.outbackfibers.com

The Weaving Works
16825 48th Ave W, Unit 130, Lynnwood,
WA 98037
www.weavingworks.com

SUNDRY SUPPLIERS

Plastic for resist templates and haberdashery
www.dunelm.com

Rubber ribbed matting
www.screwfix.com

Bag handles and forceps
www.proopsbrothers.com

Bag making supplies and haberdashers
www.macculloch-wallis.co.uk

For many items, an internet search for the specific item you require will locate suppliers local to you.

PROJECT GUIDE

INDEX

RELATED TITLES FROM CROWOOD

Creating Felt Pictures
ISBN: 978 1 84797 317 7

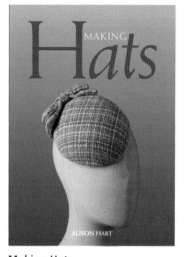

Making Hats
ISBN: 978 1 78500 493 3

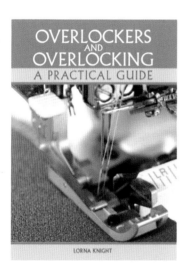

Overlockers and Overlocking
ISBN: 978 1 78500 790 3

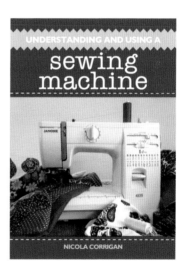

Understanding and Using a Sewing Machine
ISBN: 978 1 78500 499 5